AF413302

KNOWING IS NOT SAME AS DOING

KNOWING IS NOT SAME AS DOING

FOR ALL THE ACTION TAKERS

P.S. SATISH

Notion Press

Old No. 38, New No. 6
McNichols Road, Chetpet
Chennai - 600 031

First Published by Notion Press 2017
Copyright © P.S. Satish 2017
All Rights Reserved.

PB ISBN 978-1-947586-81-9
HC ISBN: 979-8-89475-085-9

Dedication

To my beloved mother Saraswati who was an icon
of patience.

Contents

Foreword

Based on my experience, I have concluded that the purpose of higher education is to create global citizens. A global citizen is a member of the Global Community, rather than only being the citizen of one country. A Global Citizen respects cultural diversity, globalisation, interdependence, social justice and equity, sustainable development, resolves conflicts and works towards peace. This is necessary as we are connected socially and culturally through media, telecommunications, travel and migration, economically through trade, environmentally through sharing one planet, and politically through international relations and systems of regulation. A Global Citizen should have competencies like discipline knowledge, critical thinking competence, interpersonal competence, intercultural awareness, Social/Societal engagement, or active participation at a local level and at a global level and great communication skills.

Once a person starts thinking about what his/her life is all about and how to lead a successful and happy life, he/she should start setting goals in life. Setting goals in life is a no easy task, as it needs understanding of the world around. The school, the university, parents and friends may all help – but one will have his/her own latent abilities, ideas and aspirations.

Though, in the beginning it can be a difficult task, reading motivational and inspirational books combining scientific principles and life experience, it may help in setting goals and priorities in life, in addition to interacting with the ecosystem around. Most of the successful people that the world has seen – each has a great story to narrate. Thus, there is no definite formula exists. One has to develop his or her own formula to be successful and happy in life.

Knowledge acquisition is important. But that alone will not lead to success in life unless followed by actions on it. The author of this book makes you think on this through small stories and his personal real life experiences.

The author of this book, Mr. P S Satish, is known to me for the last thirty-five years, starting from our engineering days. He was himself a great student, a great friend to everyone and has successfully worked in both the corporate world and in academics. He has international experience, and has also made an attempt to suggest the younger generation what needs to be done to be successful in life and manage life better. In our university, we have created an independent directorate to train students on transferable skills on similar lines and students are getting a better experience of life.

I recommend that university students and other graduates read this book as it might inspire, motivate them and act as a guide to setting goals for a successful and happy life.

With best wishes,

Prof (Dr.) S R Shankapal,
Vice Chancellor,
Ramaiah University of Applied Sciences,
Bengaluru.

Introduction

Why did I write this book? I had no plans to write one though I have written a few articles before. After working for the manufacturing industry for close to three decades, I left the corporate world to pursue my interest in training, teaching and mentoring individuals and companies. During this period, in many of my lectures, seminars and training sessions, I used to insist on the values of life, value-based education, the importance of taking responsibility for one's own actions, commitment to actions, etc. These were told typically with a story or an incident from my own life. One of the students once suggested that I write a book compiling my various stories. The result is that what you have in hand now.

I added action points as I believe that only actions give results. "Being" is the first step, and it should be followed by "doing." Some may feel that the lessons or values explained are obvious and are old-fashioned. No. These lessons are eternal and though they seem obvious, they are challenging to implement and sustain. The human tendency is to take small things for granted and always look for complex things.

Whether a society is good or bad is decided by the values the individual in the society believes in. These values should be inculcated in students at a college level for them to face life robustly. What is the use of a master's degree if the student does not know how to face failures in life? To build one's personality, he or she should work on many aspects and the book attempts to look at a few of them.

I have always been concerned about the gap between industries and academic institutions. Industry says that freshers have no idea of the basic things of life apart from subject knowledge. In the college syllabus, the soft skills needed for life are not dealt with in detail. Even if is done, it is done as a ritual with a higher focus on sharing knowledge. Although the college takes enormous efforts to plan and execute academic subjects, very little is done to teach students about behaviour, values, attitude and other soft aspects of life. The curriculum does not cover these and it is left to the students to learn these on their own. The assumption is that students should have learnt all these at home, which need not be the truth.

Training in the soft aspects will not give results unless an individual introspects to identify his own gap and takes action to bridge it, consistently. There is no lift to success in life. Only steps. Take one step at a time. In our current education system, high focus is on how to make a living rather than how to live to be happy. Verbal knowledge taught in college e.g. falling of the apple from a tree is due to gravity – will not help much in leading a happy and fulfilled life.

For that, transformative knowledge is required which can be learned from scriptures, life experiences, masters (gurus) and books. I strongly believe that college students and freshers who have just graduated should focus on the soft aspects as expertise in a subject alone is not enough for success in life and career. For this, they need to be provided with a structure to address the gap. The book attempts to do that.

To drive home the message that "doing" is important and that "knowing" alone is not enough, I quote a sentence from Swami Vivekananda, 'Education is not the amount of information that you put in your brain and runs riot there, undigested all your life. We must have life-building, man-making, character-making assimilation of Ideas. If you have assimilated five ideas and made them your life and character, you have more education than any man who has got by heart a whole library.'

I have enjoyed writing this book. I am grateful to all the persons who came into my life, who left me with a lesson that I can take from them. I thank all my friends, relatives and well-wishers who shared from their lives, sent to me through messages and mails. I acknowledge all the authors and thinkers whose ideas I would have used to drive home a few points.

This book is incomplete without acknowledging the support of my wife Janaki, son Sanjay and daughter Sanjana. They were patient enough to listen to my lectures and gave me invaluable suggestions.

How to Use This Book

"No amount of reading or memorising will make you successful in life. It is the understanding and application of wise thought which counts."

– Bob Proctor

I recommend that you read the book once to get a feel of what it is about. Then, start with a topic/chapter that you like. There is no specific order suggested in the reading of the chapters since each is independent. After reading a chapter, introspect to identify a few actions that you can take on that subject. Do not worry about whether it is a small or a big action. The important thing is to take action. The action could be related to change of habit, thinking or the way a particular thing is done.

The starting point of "doing" is to make the decision to take "action," with determination. Only actions will give results. When writing down the actions, try to be as specific as possible. The book is segregated into 52 chapters, so you can adopt a few actions in each chapter per week. Considering the importance of "doing" or actions, only one specific topic can be taken up per week. Follow the actions committed for the week consciously. Even an attempt to change the thinking is an action, but write it down. After three months, relook at the chapter and actions to check whether what you committed was followed. This is from the principle of P-D-C-A – namely Plan–Do–Check–Act. Follow the same pattern for the rest of the chapters.

In few chapters, you will find that you already know what is being talked about. It is good to have knowledge on this and I appreciate your knowledge. But ask yourself a question, "Have I really implemented enough to reap benefits from the things I know?" Remember that knowledge works only if you take actions. Knowledge of just ideas is useless. You cannot learn playing cricket from commentator tips. You need to get into the field and practice. Overcome your resistance to take actions.

If you are already taking a few actions against a chapter, complement yourself and continue till it becomes a habit. I recommend that you write down all the actions as they occur. Do not rely on your memory power. According to one study, the commitment level is higher when one writes things down. Also, identify the actions which you want to stop doing. To enhance the benefits, you can partner with a friend to help each other with the chapters and on actions identified.

You will get results if you demonstrate patience and perseverance and develop an attitude of "not giving up." Watch whether there is a change in your behaviour over the period. If yes, congratulations and remember, it is the result of the actions you took.

Anything is possible only if you take the first step. A big fire starts with a small spark. Start and you will master it. Keep this book with you always, to remind you of the actions you committed to and repeat your actions. Remember the words from Aristotle, "We are what we repeat."

Good luck.

Being a Member of the 99 Club

Be thankful for what you have; you will end up having more. If you concentrate on what you don't have, you will never ever have enough.

– Oprah Winfrey

One of the typical traits of the human being, which we see more of today, is the desire to acquire more and more. Greed is taking over need. There is a saying by a poet that says: pursuing things we do not have instead of enjoying what we have has become a way of life. In some way, we are becoming members of the 99 Club. You are wondering what that is? Read on to understand what I am referring to.

There was a king. He had everything life could give him – abundant wealth, a number of queens, loyal servants, a very big empire, sons and daughters, etc. In spite of all this, he was not happy. He could not sleep properly. He always had the feeling that he was missing something. The next morning, when he woke up, the barber came to give him the usual haircut. The king noticed that the barber was very happy always, involved in his work and with a smile on his face. Sometimes, the king used to feel jealous of the barber. He used to think he as a king who had everything was not happy – so how could a barber with a meagre income be happy? The king asked the barber the reason behind his perennial happiness. The barber said, "King, I am a poor man. I am blessed that I have a king like you to serve. I take care of my family by working every day. They are happy. I am not worried about tomorrow as I know that you will take care of me. I just involve myself fully in my work without worrying about anything." The king was surprised to hear this.

The king told the minister about the barber's lack of worry and perennial state of happiness. The minister replied that it was so because the barber was not a member of the 99 Club. The king did not understand this. The minister asked the king to wait for a few days.

The next night, the minister ensured that a bag full of gold coins was placed near the door of the barber's house. When the barber found the bag in the morning, he was very happy. He immediately counted the number of coins. It was 99 in number. He decided to make it a hundred and struggled day and night to earn and put aside a gold coin. He became restless and was always thinking of ways to add one more coin to make a round figure of 100.

The king noticed the change in the barber. The barber looked worried, indifferent, restless; and the smile on his face had vanished. The minister told the king what had happened. The barber had become a member of the 99 Club!

Should we become members of the 99 Club? Think it over...

Self-action Plan

Actions   **By When**

1.

2.

3.

Review after Three Months

The Desire for Recognition

There is no limit to the amount good you can do if you don't care who gets the credit.

– Ronald Reagan

We attempt to do something because we want others to recognise our efforts. People donate tube lights to temples with their names written on them. This way, other devotees can see who has donated them. But these letterings obstruct light from these tube lights.

However, there are innumerable people who work for their own satisfaction, whether someone recognises their efforts or not. They just keep on doing good things for others and the world. The famous Kannada poet Dr. G S Shivarudrappa has written a poem in which he says that a forest bird does not sing in expectation of any awards.

Here is an incident from the time of the *Ramayana*. When Sage Valmiki completed writing the great epic, Sage Narada made a comment that the *Ramayana* written by Hanuman was better than that of Valmiki.

Valmiki was surprised and was curious to see what Hanuman had written. He set out to find whose work was better. He went to the plantain farm where Hanuman was living. Hanuman shared with him the *Ramayana* that he had written on banana leaves. After reading the full work that had perfect grammar, vocabulary and melody, Valmiki started weeping. Hanuman asked why...

"Once someone reads this, no one will read mine," sobbed Valmiki. "Is that all? Don't worry about that," said Hanuman, and he tore up the banana leaves on which he had written his epic. Then he said, "Sage, you wrote *Ramayana* because you wanted the world to read and recognise it as your work. But I wrote to remember my Lord Sriram. I wrote for my own satisfaction without any expectation of recognition."

Valmiki understood his own desire for the validation and recognition of his work. Valmiki had written out of ambition, and Hanuman, out of love. That is why Hanuman's writing was better.

This is a very illuminative tale. It tells us something about ourselves on how we should recognise our actions. We need to just do the job to fulfil our bigger purpose in life, like Hanuman did. Also, looking for recognition or validation from others may affect our efforts

Let us do our best without looking for validation from others.

Self-action Plan

Actions   **By When**

1.

2.

3.

Review after Three Months

Being Proactive

One who has never made a mistake has never tried anything new.

– Albert Einstein

There are three kinds of people – the first who wait for something to happen, the second who wonder about what is happening; and the third category are those who will make it happen. The group of people belonging to the third category is preferred by every organisation or institution. How many of us take the first move to wish others good morning? Being proactive means taking the initiative without being told to do it and not being reactive.

Everyone in the court of the Emperor Akbar was jealous of the minister Birbal. The pundits in the court felt that they were more intelligent and well-read than Birbal, yet Akbar consulted only Birbal for everything. They expressed their feelings to Akbar one day, when Birbal was yet to come to court. The Emperor heard that a caravan was passing the border. He asked one of the pundits to go and find out where the caravan was coming from. The pundit scurried out and returned with the information that it was coming from Persia. The king then asked another pundit to find out to where the caravan was heading. This man returned with the information that the caravan was heading to Kabul. A third was sent to ask the name of the leader of the caravan. In this way, each of the pundits did what the Emperor asked them to do.

Now Akbar called Birbal to court and said, "I hear that a caravan has come into town…" Birbal replied, "Yes, Your Majesty. I heard about it too. So before coming to court, I went to find out the details."

He then told the Emperor where the caravan was going and who the leader was. He also said, "I found out that they were passing our border without paying the taxes. I ensured that taxes were collected and deposited in treasury."

Hearing this, the pundits felt ashamed. They realised that all they did was follow instructions. Birbal however, ensured that he was proactive and did what he had to do as a courtier. That was the reason why Akbar depended on him so much.

Proactive people are self-starters. They are not afraid of making mistakes and are the opposite of reactive people. The problem with reactive people is that their Leader or Boss has to give them instructions and follow up later. Shall we be proactive and take the first action without being told? Let us not try to be perfect and not try *not* to do mistakes. In trying to be perfect, we may not attempt many things.

Self-action Plan

Actions   **By When**

1.

2.

3.

Review after Three Months

Dare to Dream

Whatever the mind of man can conceive and believe, it can achieve.

– Napolean Hill

Every achiever talks of his or her dreams. It is nothing but having a bigger picture of life. Dr. APJ Abdul Kalam, considered the father of missile technology in India, in all his speeches, would invariably make a reference to the importance of dreaming. He used to ask every student he met a question, "What is your dream?" If the student replied that she or he did not have a dream, then his immediate suggestion would be to develop one. His famous quote on dreaming, "Dream is not something you get when you are sleeping. It is something which will not allow you to sleep." Some people call it as having a vision.

Everyone interested in the Himalaya mountains would know Tenzing Norgay. Around the age of forty, he climbed Mount Everest, the peak of the Himalaya mountains, at a height of 8,848 metres. He did this along with Edmund Hillary on the 29th of May 1953. They were the first in the world to achieve this feat. After their success, many press reporters hounded them to understand the secret of their success.

One of the reporters asked Tenzing how he felt about his achievement and what the inspiration behind his success was. The reporters were surprised to hear from Tenzing reply saying that he had resolved to climb Mount Everest when he was 10 years of age. When they asked further Tenzing said, "We are from a Sherpa family. As a boy, I used to take sheep to graze below the mountain. My mother used to tell me repeatedly that no one has climbed that tall mountain called Mount Everest." She would show Tenzing Mount Everest every day and ask him if he would climb that mountain one day. "From that day onwards, I started dreaming of climbing Mount Everest. My mother was actually the inspiration. She made me climb the mountain in my mind first. From that point onwards, I started preparing myself to climb and achieved it one day." If Tenzing's mother had told him at that young age that climbing Mount Everest would be difficult, that he would fall and injure himself, Tenzing would probably not have attempted the climb.

I once listened to a lecture by Sadhguru Jaggi Vasudev, founder of the Isha Foundation, Coimbatore, India. He dreamt of increasing the green coverage in Tamilnadu state by planting trees. He had to struggle initially to convince his disciples and his first task was to plant trees in their minds before having them physically plant them. The project became a reality and his dream materialised.

Parents and teachers have a great responsibility to create and nurture dreams in children's minds. We have heard of the influence that the mothers had in the lives of Chatrapati Shivaji, Swami Vivekananda, Mahatma Gandhiji and so on. By encouraging children to have a dream, we condition the young mind to see a bigger picture and act accordingly in life. Girish Karnad, the well-known writer in Kannada and a Jnanapeeta Awardee, writes in one of his plays, "We can live without eyes. Can we live without dreams?"

All of us should have one big picture of life and start dreaming.

Self-action Plan

Actions   **By When**

1.

2.

3.

Review after Three Months

Being Nice

You are never going to please everyone and if you do, there is something wrong.

– **Constance Wu**

Who does not like to be a "nice person"? All of us want to work with or interact with nice people. We all appreciate the popular saying, "It is nice to be important, but it's more important to be nice." Being nice and kind is considered one of the good qualities of a person. Once imbibed, niceness becomes a part of one's attitude. But being nice in all situations may not be good. By itself, "nice" does not have value unless it is demonstrated. It is like zero in mathematics. Zero, the great invention of Indians, by itself has no value. But the value comes by its position with numbers. Whether it appears before and after a number, makes a big difference. The addition of each zero after a number, increases its value exponentially. In some situations, niceness adds value immensely; but in a few others, it may not help or may even impact negatively.

There was once a ferocious cobra. Everyone was naturally afraid of it and no one dared to come near it.

Because of this it didn't have any friends. It once went to a saint and explained its problem to him. The saint advised the snake to be nice and kind to everyone. From that day on, the cobra decided not to bite anyone. The next day, a few urchins were playing near the anthill where the snake lived. During the game, they sensed that the snake was harmless and nice, and they took advantage of it. They started teasing it and even tortured by using the snake as a rope in one their games. Its body writhing in pain, the snake went to the saint and explained what had happened. The saint said, "My dear snake, I told you to be nice. But I did not tell you to keep quiet when someone harms or ill-treats you. You could have at least hissed at the urchins to protect yourself."

People who are nice, definitely conquer others' hearts and are bound to be popular. But like the snake in the story, being too nice could be a negative trait and others could take advantage of this. Some take nice people for granted. Others may think of them as naïve, as fools, without commonsense and as people who are not shrewd. Being too good to everybody and all the time may be a negative quality. In management jargon, there is a phrase called "situational leadership." When we talk of leadership, we consider it good when a leader consults everyone before taking a decision. But this approach can be negative in some situations like when there is a fire in the company. In such situations, the leader has to be commanding to get work done. That means, that the leadership style should change according to the situation. Similarly, the extent of niceness may need to change depending on the situation and type of people being dealt with. People who want to appear nice, are likely to pretend to look good to others. They have a problem saying "No" and end up doing a lot of work for others, putting aside their own priority or goal.

To what extent should we be nice?

Self-action Plan

Actions   **By When**

1.

2.

3.

Review after Three Months

Engaging in Social Service

Do what you can, with what you have, where you are.

– Theodore Roosevelt

All of us are social animals. We have to live in society, helping each other and supporting the environment in which we live. If we live only for ourselves, it would be selfish thinking. As human beings, we should live and help others. We all earn for a living. We get some form of compensation for the work we do. Can't we not do some form of work for society or for others, and not expect anything in return?

Thimmakka was a woman from a small village of Karnataka. She wanted to make a difference to society. Many banyan trees were growing near her village. She started taking saplings of the trees to further plant on the sides of a nearby highway. She started with ten samplings and increased the numbers, until she finally planted 384 banyan trees. She and her husband used to water and take care of the plants till they reached a reasonable size. She protected the saplings from cattle, with a fence of thorny bushes. She took care of the trees like they were her own children. She did all this without expecting any returns or recognition for her work. She planted trees for four kilometres along the highway. The trees would not only give shelter, but would also support the environment. Society and the government noticed her noble work and a lot of awards and recognitions came her way. She is popularly now known as Salumarada (row of trees) Thimmakka.

A senior citizen in Bangalore decided to do social service in a unique way. He would get up early in the morning and go to a place near his house, where newspaper boys segregate the various newspapers. He would collect all the white papers that were used to cover the bundles of papers. He would then cut those papers at home to prepare rough note books that could be used by students. He distributed these notebooks to boys who studied in the government school nearby. His act was not just to save the environment, but it helped the school students too.

A former president of the USA famously said, "Ask not what country has done for you. Ask first what you have done for the country." We take so much from society from the day we are born and we are duty-bound to give back in whatever way we can. To serve society does not mean that we should sacrifice everything of ourselves. Even talking positive about society, encouraging and guiding others to do good work, is also a form of social service. According to Swami Vivekananda, service to society is a great form of worship to God. He said that spirituality without service has no meaning. We find many people engaged in social service only for the sake of recognition. That is not considered good social service. There are plenty of great people who have sacrificed their lives for a social cause. Examples like Mahatma Gandhi, Vivekananda, Martin Luther King and so many others come to mind. For them, living for others and society was the purpose of life.

Shall we start thinking of what we can do for society?

Self-action Plan

Actions   **By When**

1.

2.

3.

Review after Three Months

Leaving the Comfort Zone

There are risks and costs to action. But they are far less than the long range risks of comfortable inaction.

– John F. Kennedy

The human tendency is to stay in a comfort zone. Have you seen people who stay in a company without any potential to grow, only because it's a comfort zone? They would have got used to the comfort level so much that they resist any possibility of change. The actual opportunity lies outside the comfort zone. When the comfort zone is established, the stronger the force required to pull you out of the comfort zone. We know the saying, "If you want to stay on the shore of the sea without sailing, you will miss the beauty of the other side."

Once there was a king who received two magnificent falcons as gifts from another king. They were very beautiful. The king gave the birds to his head falconer to train them. After a few months, the falconer informed the king that though one bird was flying majestically and soaring high in the sky, the other bird had not moved from its perch since the day it arrived.

The king summoned many experts to check on the bird, but no one could understand the problem. When all attempts failed, the king brought in a farmer who was familiar with dealing with falcons, to look into the problem.

The next day, to the king's surprise, the bird which had so far resisted moving, was soaring high above the palace. The king was curious to know how the farmer had made the bird fly. "It was very easy Your Highness," said the farmer, bowing low, "I simply cut the branch on which the bird was sitting."

Many a time, we sit on the branch clinging to things familiar to us, though we have the potential to fly high. The routine makes us comfortable and any change brings stress. The possibilities and opportunities then, will remain undiscovered. We will remain in our comfort zones. To soar high, we need get out of our comfort zone. The branch of comfort should be cut down.

Shall we look at the opportunities we are losing in our attempt to remain in the comfort zone?

Self-action Plan

Actions   **By When**

1.

2.

3.

Review after Three Months

How Well Do We Engage in Our Work?

When people go to work, they shouldn't have to leave their hearts at home.

– Betty Bender

Many a time, we engage in work half-heartedly. We may be working for a Boss or an Employer just to fulfil the basic need of the job, without too much involvement. We think that we should not struggle too much when the results or benefit of our work goes to someone else. What we get at the end of the day because of our mediocre work will not be good. "As you sow, so you reap," is an apt saying here.

A highly skilled carpenter who had grown old decided to take voluntary retirement from his employment with a builder. He told his boss of his plans to leave the job. He wanted to take rest and spend more time with his family. He would miss the monthly salary, but he wanted to balance out his life by taking voluntary retirement. The boss was sorry to see an excellent worker leave and asked if he could work on just one more house as a personal favour. The carpenter agreed to this. He didn't want to say no the boss who had been good to him.

So, he began work on the house. In retirement mode, he didn't pay too much attention to detail. His heart was not in his work. He was in a hurry to complete the job and retire. He resorted to poor workmanship and used inferior materials. When the job was done, the boss called the carpenter over to the house and handed over some papers and the key to him. "This is your house, my gift to you for having served this company for so many years," the boss said.

The carpenter was in shock. What a shame. If only he had known that he was building his own house, he would have done a better job with good materials.

Many a time, we are in a situation similar to that of the carpenter. If we do a job half-heartedly, chances are that the work will rebound on us. God wills it that we get the best – but sometimes, we ourselves put a spoke in it by not giving our best.

Good work always gives good results.

Shall we resolve to engage fully in all the things we do?

Self-action Plan

Actions   **By When**

1.

2.

3.

Review after Three Months

Other People's Problems

A Leader must be a good listener. He must be willing to take counsel.
He must show a genuine concern and love for those under his
stewardship.

– James Faust

In organisations and in society, people do not respond or are unconcerned about others' problems thinking that it no way affects them. We do not realise that one issue or problem in the system slowly affects us at some point of time. In an apartment, if one house has problem, say a leaky tap, it will affect everyone staying in the apartment directly or indirectly. The normal reaction of looking at others' problem is to sympathise or feel pity and not do anything about it.

In a farmer's house, there was a pig, a chicken and a cow. These animals were living together happily and were well taken care of by the farmer. There was also a rat in the house which had developed friendship with the other animals. One day, the rat noticed that the farmer had bought a rat-trap from the market. It got frightened and could not sleep that night thinking that its life was numbered. The rat wanted to share its problem with the other animal friends to get a possible solution. First it went to the chicken. The chicken said, "Oh Rat, I really pity your situation. Enjoy what life is left. I am safe from this." Next, the rat went to the pig to see if he would help. The pig said, "My dear friend. You are a good animal. I do not know why problems come only to good people. I pray for your life. I recommend that you also pray." Next, the rat went to the cow. The cow said, "Mr. Rat, you are in real danger. You really have to do something about it. I am safe as the farmer wants my milk every day." Frustrated with the answers from his three friends, the rat started cursing his fate. It so happened that night, the farmer's wife heard a noise from the rat-trap. It was dark and she could not see the trap fully. She got bitten by a snake whose tail had got stuck in the trap. She fell ill and became very weak. The doctor advised that she drink chicken soup to get better soon. The chicken was therefore killed and made into soup.

As she was ill, many friends and family came to visit. The pig fell victim to this situation. The farmer butchered him and fed the visitors. One day, his wife died. Now all the visitors to the funeral needed to be fed – the cow was therefore butchered too.

Finally, only the rat survived. If only the friends had given him a solution to the trap, they would have survived too

When we hear of someone's problem, let us not ignore it thinking that we are not involved. Let us help them with a solution. What do you think?

Self-action Plan

Actions   **By When**

1.

2.

3.

Review after Three Months

Interpersonal Relationships

We can improve many relationships if we understand a simple fact that people are not wrong but different.

– Anonymous

Building relationships is an art. According to one theory, Resources + Relationship = Results. What this means is that results will be enhanced with good usage of resources along with relationship as an important ingredient. In a team, if interpersonal relationships among members is not healthy, the results from the team efforts will not be up to the mark.

I narrate a story I heard at one seminar. A woman had problems with her husband. To get peace of mind, she went to a teacher. "Teacher, I have been married for a few years. My husband finds fault with everything I do. He is always occupied in his own work, and finds no time for me. I think he does not love me. How do I make him love me?" The teacher replied, "I can give you a medicine to cure your problem. But I have an issue. I don't have stock of one of the ingredients needed for the preparation of the medicine. I need the hair of lion. If you can get it, your issue will be resolved." The woman had no clue as to how to get the hair of a lion. But she did not want to give up as she badly wanted a solution. She went to the forest searching for lion but in vain. Later, she took a leg of mutton with her to the forest thinking that a lion may be attracted by the smell and find her. Finally, a lion came by. Afraid of its appearance, she fled the forest. The next day she returned with the mutton, but this time, summoned the courage to offer it to the lion. The lion however, did not come near at all. This happened for a few days. At last, one day, the lion came close and took the mutton from her. After months of such feeding, the lion began to trust her, and one day, she was able to pluck a few hairs from his mane. Elated, she ran to the teacher with them. He just threw them away. The woman was shocked. She wept, telling him the kind of effort she had put into getting the hair.

The teacher said, "If only you had demonstrated the patience, love and faith that you gave to the animal, with your husband, would he not have loved you by now?"

A lot of time is required to build interpersonal relationships. Without any efforts from our side, no relationship will materialise. When we talk of investment, we only think of money. To build interpersonal relationships, we need to invest time. Nothing comes free.

Should we not invest time and effort to build interpersonal relationships?

Self-action Plan

Actions   **By When**

1.

2.

3.

Review after Three Months

Grow Bigger Than Problems

Who does not have problems and challenges? The magnitude may vary. Even a monk faces these. It is sometimes an irony that while solving problems, people get into new ones. The famous automobile manufacturer Toyota declares that problems are welcome and encourages their employees not to desist or shy away from them. Their logic is, that problem-solving will make the system or product more robust. Instead of worrying about problems, we should grow bigger than the problem, so that the problem is not perceived as a threat or a stumbling block.

In the great epic *Mahabharata*, there is an incident. Lord Krishna and his brother Balarama were once travelling through a forest. It became dark and they had to spend the night there. They came to an agreement that they would take turns sleeping and waking every few hours. Krishna went to sleep first. Balarama was strolling about when he encountered a *rakshasa* (demon). Terrified by the giant creature, Balarama screamed aloud and fainted. Hearing the scream, Krishna woke up. He saw Balarama lying down and thought he was sleeping. He decided to keep watch.

The *rakshasa* now attacked Krishna. Krishna made himself bigger and bigger till finally, the monster was tiny in comparison. He picked up the monster and tied him to a corner of his upper cloth. At dawn, Balarama came to his senses and woke up. The brothers started walking towards town.

Balarama told Krishna all about the *rakshasa*. Krishna smiled and unknotted a corner of his upper cloth to show Balarama the *rakshasa*, who was now a tiny figure.

When you avoid problems or challenges, they become bigger than you. You must take control of them. When you are ready to face a problem, you become bigger than it. As you grow bigger, the problem becomes smaller and you can handle it better.

The magnitude of the problem is relative. If you allow it to grow bigger than you, you cannot control it.

Let us grow bigger than our problems and challenges, and take control of them.

Self-action Plan

Actions	By When
1.	
2.	
3.	

Review after Three Months

Knowing versus Doing

I have been impressed with the urgency of doing. Knowing is not enough, we must apply. Being willing is not enough, we must do.

– Leonardo da Vinci

In my trainings, I insist on the importance of knowing things first before doing them. Having said that, only focusing on the knowing without applying what is known is a waste of time. The mind is not a space just to store information. It should work on processing the information acquired through knowing. There is a saying, "A pinch of application is worth tonnes of abstraction." The possession of knowledge does not mean that one is going to use it. Even an attempt to apply what is learnt gives good dividend. Let me tell you a story I read in Wayne Dyer's book, simplified with minor modifications for better understanding:

Long ago there was a monk in China who used to sit on top of the branches of different trees for meditation each day. He was said to be very intelligent and had the ability to guide people in overcoming their problems. The blowing wind, the blazing sun or even the shake of the tree did not disturb him. Villagers who passed by whichever tree he was seated on, used to take advice from him for their problems. The reputation of the monk grew all over the province. The local Governor came to know of the monk and decided to consult him for an important matter. Since the monk changed trees each day, it was tough for people to locate him. The Governor went in search of the monk and finally located him. "Monk, I am the Governor of this province. I have a question to ask you, for which I haven't found an answer so far. I want to know the most important thing Buddha said." After a while, the monk, without opening his eyes said, "Governor, don't do bad things. Always do good things. This was the important message of Buddha." The Governor was a little disappointed with his answer and said, "Monk, I have taken a lot of pain to locate you. For that, you are giving me such a simple answer to my question! Even a child knows what you just told me!"

The monk replied, "I know that even a child knows this, but still eighty-year-old people find it difficult to do. Knowing is not enough. Please implement what you know already." The Governor understood the message and left.

Knowing is not the same thing as doing. Both are different. A pot of knowledge without application is a waste.

Let us start doing what we know.

Self-action Plan

Actions   **By When**

1.

2.

3.

Review after Three Months

Lesson from the Japanese

Better than a thousand days of diligent study, is one day with a great Teacher.

– Japanese proverb

I have observed that many good practices of the Japanese have crept into manufacturing. We have seen many MBA schools teach Japanese management as a subject of study. The focus on discipline, ownership, pride about the country, teamwork, thinking about continuous improvements, and housekeeping, makes the Japanese special. These qualities have made them successful globally. I had a few opportunities to work with the Japanese and I cite here three examples from my experience that we can learn from:

⇨ I have been working with a Japanese for a long time as a business partner. In one of his visits to Bangalore, we went to a coffee shop in Bangalore for a meeting. He observed a coffee stain on the table where we took our seats. He went to the counter, picked up a napkin, and wiped off the stain. He did not request for the service person to come and clean it. He demonstrated that if we observe that something is not right, we have to take the initiative to correct it first.

⇨ I once had a visitor from a Japanese company. This person wanted to smoke in between a meeting. He stepped out into a non-smoking area and started smoking. He ensured that all the ashes of the cigarette were collected in his cigarette packet, He also put the butt of his smoked cigarette into the packet. He then put it in his pocket. Since there were no ash trays, he did not want to litter or dirty the area. He demonstrated ownership in keeping the workplace clean.

⇨ I was a coordinator for a few companies from Japan who participated in an exhibition in Bangalore. The companies brought their machines, tools and other samples to demonstrate to potential customers at the exhibition. Each stall in-charge had come fully prepared with tapes, glue, staples, etc. On the last day of the show, they ensured that all the places were cleaned, the tapes removed, neatly-packed, unwanted papers thrashed in the dustbin, etc. Once they were done, the place looked cleaner than when they had taken it. The local organisers were surprised. In the opposite row, there were stalls from China. At the end of the show, that area was littered with papers,, used paper plates, unused pamphlets and was a mess. Here again, the Japanese demonstrated their ownership for keeping the place clean.

Is there a lesson for us from the Japanese?

Self-action Plan

Actions   **By When**

1.

2.

3.

Review after Three Months

Keeping Oneself Charged

When you buy a smart phone, what do you look for? You would go for the brand, the size, the software, etc. and importantly, battery life. You would want a battery with a higher capacity and which will charge fast, so that you do not need to charge it frequently. It is an unimaginable situation when a call is disconnected for want of charge. As a backup, today you have the option of a power bank. Compared to the earlier phones, today's smart phone consumes more power and requires to be charged regularly.

Is there a similarity between charging a battery and charging yourself? The answer is definitely yes. Like a battery, you need to charge yourself. Without energy, you get drained fast and your work will suffer. How do you charge yourself then? I give a few suggestions here:

⇨ Get up early in the morning and spend some time in meditation or in introspection to prepare your mind to face the tasks or challenges of the day. Mental preparation is very important. The way the first step is important for the athlete; the start of the day decides the course of the day.

⇨ Read a portion of good book often. It could be on philosophy, motivation, the life story of successful people or a book on personality development. Good thoughts taken from the book keep your mind energised.

⇨ Prayer is the best connector for charging oneself.

⇨ Spend some time in a week in a Satsang, listening to a good lecture, watching motivational videos, or readings similar books. Develop friendships with positive people.

⇨ Walking helps in overcoming stress and it is good if you walk in the company of like-minded people.

⇨ Engage in a game or a physical activity you like, regularly.

⇨ Music is wonderful therapy for relaxation of the mind. Listen to music you like.

⇨ Spending some time with oneself in silence, if possible with minimal thoughts, will charge the mind.

⇨ Doing yoga, including breathing exercises (*Pranayama*) daily has effect on the body, mind, energy and emotions.

⇨ Always eat good food. Junk food is known to add carbohydrates and fat without the required proteins, nutrients and vitamins. Let fruits and vegetables be part of what you eat daily.

⇨ Positive thinking is always a wonderful charger to the mind. This does not mean that you expect only positive things, but means that you accept any situations in the best possible way.

⇨ Learn to accept things as they come. You can try to change a situation. If you cannot, simply accept it. Grumbling means discharging of energy. Do not complain if you cannot do anything to change the situation.

⇨ Stress drains your mind quickly. Managing stress does not mean escaping; but coping with a smile and an effort to change the root cause.

⇨ Be selective in watching TV and videos. Engage constructively in social media.

A ship floats in water and is surrounded by it. It will not sink unless it allows the water to get in. Our mind in today's world, is surrounded by uncertainty, complexity, ambiguity, volatility... Practising a few of the above points daily, at least for an hour, will shield your mind for the next 23 hours. We will be in a "charged" condition always.

Are you ready to start?

Self-action Plan

Actions   **By When**

1.

2.

3.

Review after Three Months

The Effect of Ego

When nails grow long, we cut nails and not fingers. Similarly, when misunderstandings grow, cut your ego and not your relationship.

– Anonymous

You must have encountered people who think only about themselves and feel that nothing moves without them. We see them in organisations, in families, in institutions and in the government. Such people do not think of collective efforts but want recognition for themselves from others. Teamwork fails with such people. Have you heard of the story of the old lady in a village who had a rooster and who used to think that the sun would rise only when her rooster crowed? Everyone in the village laughed at her thinking. Angry and to teach them a lesson, she left the village with the rooster one day, thinking that now the sun would not rise in the village, without her rooster crowing.

When she returned a few days later, she was surprised to see that life was as usual in the village.

There was the little oil lamp made of clay. The family used to light the lamp for festivals. Oil would be poured into the lamp and a wick placed, and a matchstick would be used to light it.

One day, among these four friends, there was an argument as to who was the most important. The lamp said, "I hold the oil and the wick." The oil said, "Without me, you cannot even light up." The wick said, "Oh, then? What's the use of your two without me?" The matchstick said, "Without me, you three would be useless."

They began a quarrel in earnest. In the process, the lamp broke. The oil poured out, the wick fell out and the matchstick truly became useless now. If only they had remained friends, the light would now be burning...

Light itself is a symbol of removal of darkness. Darkness is in the form of ego, selfishness, jealousy, hatred, anger, etc.

Shall we light a lamp within us to remove our inner darkness?

Self-action Plan

Actions   **By When**

1.

2.

3.

Review after Three Months

Our True Nature

– Albert Camus

There are few things that we can learn from nature. The coconut tree yields coconut, husk, and other useful material whether we use it or not. You may not take care of the tree, but it survives nevertheless and does not change its nature. The fish cannot be taught to climb a tree. It is against its nature. If we follow our nature, we can grow. Imitating others may not be beneficial.

A Zen guru had two disciples. One day, the guru told one of his disciples to fast and did not tell the other one to do anything. When the fasting disciple saw the other disciple eating food, he felt jealous and started wondering why the guru had discriminated between them. He could not ask the guru the reason and kept quiet for a few days. Weeks passed and one day, he could not hold back any longer. He asked his guru, "Teacher, is it right that you tell one disciple to fast and allow the other to eat delicious food? May I know the reason for this discrimination?"

The guru said, "Alright. You can eat what your friend is eating from tomorrow but be silent for three days. Then come and see me." The next day, the fasting disciple could not wait for the food. As soon as he was served, he gobbled the food up. But to his shock, he found it very spicy. He drank a lot of water but could not eat anymore. His friend calmly ate as usual.

Three days later, the fasting friend met the guru as promised. The guru asked him what he had learnt. "O, Teacher! Eating spicy food is natural for my friend and is his nature but not mine. I learnt a great lesson of Zen philosophy – that we should live as per our nature."

Let's take a long, hard look at ourselves. Many times, we are frustrated, jealous and angry because we do not live according to our nature. We try to live for others, putting on a mask. If we understand our own nature and engage ourselves accordingly, we will be more joyful. Trying to be like Sachin Tendulkar, Asha Bhosle or Steve Jobs, if it's not in our nature, is like chasing a mirage in a desert, making our life hell. I quote here a message I received from a friend: "Life is like an examination. In order to pass the examination, many try to copy answers from others. They do not realise that each person in life has a different question paper."

Let us explore our true nature...

Self-action Plan

Actions   **By When**

1.

2.

3.

Review after Three Months

Nurturing Friendship

Friendship is delicate as a glass bowl. Once broken it can be fixed but there will always be cracks.

– Ahmed Waqrwaqar

Good friendships are really wonderful. We can share all the ups and downs of our life with friends. Even secrets which cannot be shared with parents or spouse, can be shared with friends. Friendship is something which has to be nurtured continuously, without any mutual expectations. It is not enough to send someone greeting cards or messages once a year on Friendship Day. Besides, misuse of friendship is a no-no.

In one of the forums that I spoke, I met Rama Rao (name changed). He was well-dressed and was the first to introduce himself. He had done an MBA and had experience in the software industry, including a few years overseas. He was quick in communication and always boasted of contacts at high levels in the corporate and government institutions. He spoke about his tie-up with an institution in Australia to bring some training expertise to India.

Our acquaintance slowly turned into a friendship. We used to meet regularly at our homes to explore new opportunities. I considered him a friend, beyond business. One day, I told him that I wanted to get a good laptop for my son. He suggested a few models I could consider. After a few days, he said that a cousin of his was working in Dubai in Dell, and as an employee, he was eligible to get 2–3 laptops at 50% the price. If I wished, he would ask his cousin for a laptop for my son. Since this was a good offer, I paid the full price of the laptop in advance to him.

A few weeks later, I reminded him about the laptop. He said it was in process. Then I went off on vacation. When I returned, he said that the laptop had come to the house by courier and had been returned as the house was locked. A few months passed. Each time, he gave some excuse for the delay. I became suspicious about this and a year passed. I asked him to refund the money. He reluctantly returned a part of it, after many follow-ups. But that was the end of our friendship.

Money is like a rubber ball and friendship is like a crystal ball. If the rubber ball falls, it will bounce back. But the crystal ball, once broken, is gone. I remember a message I read somewhere on the effect of telling lie: "I am not worried that you told me lie. I am concerned that you will lose my trust."

Let us nurture good friendships and not misuse them for our selfish reasons.

Self-action Plan

Actions   **By When**

1.

2.

3.

Review after Three Months

Beyond Challenges

My ability is greater than my disability.

– Nikki Rowe

If there is one person who can limit our capability, it is ourselves. We put a restriction in our minds, in deciding our unseen boundaries, beyond which we dare not move. However, we also know people with disabilities who have crossed such boundaries easily.

There is a company called ORBIT in Thiruchirapalli, Tamilnadu, India. Here, blind people work together to make parts for boilers and supply to BHEL (a public sector company in India). The person heading the company is blind and the entire team is blind too. Though we often hear of schools and institutions for the blind, we rarely come across a manufacturing company run by visually impaired people.

The employees here have perfect synchronisation among themselves. The fabrication process involves cutting, shearing, punching of sheet metal including quality checks. They do tough jobs like welding, with another blind person as a helper. The entire process is efficiently managed, meeting high quality standards. The collective effort is amazing.

Communication among them seems seamless. Each person knows the layout of the factory and takes calculated steps to move from one place to another. The rhythm of work and its calm execution is amazing. Trainees are also blind and they are trained by the others.

ORBIT is an example that demonstrates that nothing is impossible. For those of us who have all our senses intact, would we be able to achieve such perfection?

At the age of 18, Ramona Pierson joined the marines and started writing algorithms to guide F-18 Fighters. At the age of 22, she met with a terrible accident in which both her legs were crushed, her throat and chest were ripped open. She was in coma for 18 months and was fed through a hole in the chest. She also become blind. In next two years, she underwent close to 100 surgeries. Her never-say-die attitude had her complete master's degree in psychology and a doctorate in neuroscience at the age of 27. After 11 years being blind, she regained sight in her left eye through a miraculous operation. Later, she supported soldiers returning from the Middle East and developed software. She started a technology company called Declara that offered social networking with AI. Here, what I am pointing out, is that Pierson became successful despite so many odds. She never gave up and her disability didn't stop her.

We have seen many people with lesser disabilities cursing their fate and doing nothing about it. ORBIT and Pierson are examples to all. The human mind is capable of the unimaginable. Winning odds amidst challenges gives us all the courage to move forward.

Shall we resolve to go beyond our challenges?

Self-action Plan

Actions   **By When**

1.

2.

3.

Review after Three Months

The Purpose of Business

The blind pursuit of profit at all costs is untenable. It is essential that we make money the right way. After all, if communities suffer as a result of company's actions, those returns are not sustainable.

– Indra K Nooyi

All of are in business in some way or the other. When we say business, trading and commercial activities is what comes to mind. However, my reference here is not restricted to these alone. I speak about our professions, careers, jobs, vocations and many more things. For example, I am in the "speaking" business. My old classmate is a priest in a temple and he is in the "worshipping" business. In whatever business we are in, we should have clarity of purpose.

A leading doctor saw an opportunity to open a hospital in the small town where he was born. He built a very good facility in his home town. He requested a famous spiritual leader to inaugurate the hospital. The spiritual leader asked the doctor what he should do at the inauguration. The doctor said, "Swamiji, there is no bigger hospital in my town, with the facilities we offer. I am sure everyone in town will make use of my new hospital. You should come and bless me so that I make more profits." The leader replied, "Doctor, what you are telling me is that I should come and pray for more illness in people. Only then will your profit increase. I am sorry, I cannot do that." The doctor was disappointed. But the spiritual leader said, "Doctor, I will come. But I will not bless you so that you increase your profit. Instead, I bless you to give you more strength to serve sick people and needy ones. The purpose of your business should be to wipe out the diseases of people and profit is but a corollary. Hope you will agree." The doctor was happy – the spiritual leader had given him a better focus in life and business.

For example, if you are running a catering service, the purpose can be to provide healthy food along with good service. Here, focusing only on money is likely to bring down the quality of food and service which will not sustain in the long term. Endamuri Veerendranath, a famous novel writer in the Telugu language once said in answer to a question on why he writes, "I do not write for money or fame. I write because I want to convey my idea to readers and that gives me joy." No doubt he is very popular and has also made money and got fame. In the short term, any business can thrive; but for the long term, clarity of purpose gives a clear direction. If we focus on the bigger purpose, then money is automatically the by-product.

In the corporate world, purpose is defined by a Mission statement.

Have we defined the purpose of our business?

Self-action Plan

Actions   **By When**

1.

2.

3.

Review after Three Months

Management of the Self

There is nothing so useless as doing efficiently that which should not be done at all.

– Peter Drucker

In the corporate world, management is about setting objectives, organising, controlling, motivating, communicating, measuring and developing people within the organisation. Management in the outer world is focusing mostly on managing people. In the outer world, the target of management is to increase the Return of Investment (ROI). That means, how we get more returns from the investments made.

Investment may be in the form of infrastructure, facilities, money, effort and time. But here, I am referring to the inner world. Though geographically we have one world, inside each one of us, we have a different world. To be successful in the outside world, we must manage our inner world well. ROI is applicable for inner world management too. ROI here, could be in the form of happiness, peace, fulfilment, etc. and the inputs are our efforts, practice, time and so on. Let us look at a few ways of increasing the ROI of our inner world by better management of the self.

What we usually do is focus on the outer world by devoting time for reviews, audits and strategy to meet the objectives set. When it is related to our personal improvements in the inner world, we do not have the time, patience and will to practice. So one reason for missing progress in our inner world could be because of the rat race we are in, in blindly following what others are doing. According to Socrates, the touchstone of wisdom is to first know thyself.

A TV channel once got the head of the rat group for an interview. The rat was impatient as it could see other rats running here and there while it was sitting. The interview started. The interviewer started with the first question, "Where you are coming from?" The head said, "From the same place where the others are coming." The second question was, "Where are you going?" The reply was, "Where the other rats are going." Third question was, "Why are you running?" The head said, "Because the others are running. How can I sit when the others are progressing by running?" He became impatient and started looking at his watch. Then he said, "Do not waste my time further. I have to run." He ran away to join the other rats. Our inner development will not happen when we do not pause and get out of the rat race instead.

Humans prayed to God, "Why are you giving us so many problems. Please give us a way to happiness." God listened, showed them a locked box and said, "The secret of happiness lies inside this box. Go and search for the key." Humans searched the earth, the sea and space looking for the key. In desperation, they returned to God. God asked, "Did you search your heart? The key to happiness is inside you and you search for it everywhere other than your inner self. That is the reason for all your problems."

Success has different meanings for different people. For me, success is when we realise our full potential. It is closing the gap between what we are doing and what we can do. The gap is the measure of success in our inner world. To be successful within, we need to put in a hundred percent in the job we are doing now, in the present without worrying about the past and thinking about the future. Stop worrying about things we cannot control, and start living.

When we buy a gadget, we are always updating the software to improve the capability of the gadget. But we do not bother to update the inner software in our mind. We try to manage new things with the old software. Let us upgrade ourselves with new skills and new ways of thinking as we grow in age with experience.

To manage ourselves, we should stop trying to control others and the world. By controlling ourselves, others will look at us and follow.

Life is like an ECG graph. It has ups and downs. If it becomes flat, we are dead. Let us learn to enjoy the ups and downs with ease. Life is not a straight line and is full of unpredictability. We cannot change *Prarabda* (Fate) but we can modify that by *Purushartha* (Efforts). For many things that happened to us beyond our control, instead of asking the question of why it happened to me, let us focus on how do deal with it effectively.

Shall we try managing our inner selves better, keeping the inherent nature of happiness (*Ananda*), in mind?

Self-action Plan

Actions   **By When**

1.

2.

3.

Review after Three Months

Our Conduct

Circumstances are beyond human control, but our conduct is
in our own power.

– Benjamin Disraeli

In the sacred book, the *Bhagavad Gita*, there is a verse that talks about how our conduct in life should be. It can be loosely translated to, "The path taken by great and wise people will be followed by others. Whatever they believe as ideal, others will accept."

People follow or imitate others who they consider as great, as it is an easy route. Instead of searching for their own ways, they look for someone who has found a way already. Imitating is human nature. Great people are like engines who will take along with them, many bogies.

Who is great and worthy of following? For a disciple, the teacher is great. For children, parents are great. The human mind is such that it tries to imitate others even without its own knowledge. Imitation is very high in children. Have you seen children trying to sit like the father, trying to behave like the mother? All of us are great to someone who is following us. So we have the moral responsibility to conduct ourselves so that we take others on the right path. We need to follow those things which we expect from our children, since they will be looking at what we do.

I narrate here an incident in the life of Dr. Arun Gandhi, grandson of Mohandas Karamchand Gandhi. I heard about this in a lecture some time back. Dr. Arun Gandhi related, "We were staying in a village near Durban, South Africa. I was young at that time. One day, I went to the city to buy things my mother needed. Father was working in the city. I had a holiday that day. So he told me to get the car repaired and come to his office by 5 pm. There was an English movie running in the city. It was my favourite movie. I left the car in the garage and went for the movie. I quite forgot to go to my father's office by 5 pm. When I went there at 6pm. Father was anxious and asked reason for my delay. To escape, I told him a lie that the garage had delayed. But he knew the truth as he had phoned the garage by 5 pm. He did not scold me but told me, "I have erred somewhere in your upbringing that you feel the need to lie to me. The mistake lies in me and let me reflect on that while I walk home. You come by car." Then he walked the long distance back home. I never ventured to tell a lie thereafter."

Good conduct is what parents can gift their children. If each one of us conduct ourselves well, society will be good as well.

Self-action Plan

Actions   **By When**

1.

2.

3.

Review after Three Months

Lessons from a Friend's Life

People tend to complicate their own lives, as if living weren't already complicated enough.

– Carlos Ruiz Zafon

Life is a great teacher. It teaches us many things. But we need to be sensitive enough to pick up those lessons. Unlike in school, in life, there is an examination first and later a lesson. This examination could be in the form of a tough situation, a scenario and an incident. We can look for lessons every day in our day-to-day lives. Clever is the one who picks up these lessons and adopts them his own life.

I give here a few lessons I have picked up from the life of my one of my family friends. His name was Bheema (name changed). He expired at the age of 60 and suffered in many ways, the few months before his death. He accumulated huge properties in the form of lands and unfortunately lost his wife one year earlier to his death. She also suffered for a few years, with cancer. Their daughter was sixteen-years-old when he died.

⇨ *How much is enough?*

Every one of us wishes to have things in abundance. It is great to have things for a comfortable life. But at some point, we need to put a limit to what we want to possess and how much. As Gandhiji said, there is always a limit for need but not for greed. Bheema never put a full stop his pursuit of acquisition till the end of his life.

⇨ *Ignoring the warnings*

Most of the time, we do get a warning for an upcoming situation. Many a time, we ignore them. If we act at the first instance, many bad situations can be avoided. Many things in life happen slowly. We should be sensitive to recognise these changes. For example, complications because of a diabetic situation will not happen overnight. Exceptions can be in the form of accidents. Bheema neglected signals of his deteriorating health.

⇨ *Taking others' advise and help*

It is foolishness if one thinks that he can do everything without others' help. If not directly, indirectly, all of us have taken others' help or advice. There is no shame in asking for advice or help. We should overcome our ego to ask. Bheema did not seek anyone's advice though many were willing to help.

⇨ *Be ready to accept the inevitable*

All of us know that there is an end day to our lives. As we progress, we should prepare ourselves to accept the hard reality of our destiny. We also do not have control over others' lives. When there is a bereavement of a close relative, there will be grief, but we should accept the hard reality. Bheema never accepted his wife's death and remained under the illusion that she would come back. He suffered because of this.

⇨ *Accept the responsibility*

When we raise children, it is our responsibility to take care of them, till they are independent. We also should plan for any eventuality. Bheema never took on the responsibility for the future of his daughter. With deteriorating health, he had an opportunity to plan for her studies. He just escaped that responsibility.

⇨ *Attitude of gratitude*

We should be thankful for everything we have. Unknown hands are helping us every day. We should develop an attitude of thanking everyone in our life for helping us. Bheema lived as though others were meant to help him; but he did not bother to reciprocate their giving. The sacrifices of the elders of the family for the land were not appreciated.

⇨ *Postponing decisions*

We are there today in a way because of our past decisions. We need to take decisions continuously and sometime tough ones are needed. If not decisive, someone will else or fate will take its own course. Bheema postponed taking many decisions regarding the property including his own health check-up, waiting for a good day. Unfortunately, that day never came.

⇨ *Sharing information*

Knowing uncertainty of life, we should share with someone whom we trust, much of our thinking, wishes including information of liabilities, documents, money matters, etc. This is with an idea that the successors should not suffer because of our lapse. This should be done when one is healthy and fit. Bheema kept many secrets to himself till the end and others had to struggle later for lack of information.

⇨ *Trust people*

Trust is the foundation of our life. By trusting, there may be a few cases of problems. But by not trusting people, we will have more problems. We should have at least a few trusted people with whom we can share our problems. Bheema failed to trust people and even doubted relatives who genuinely helped him. It should not be a blind trust without proper assessment. He trusted few friends blindly who betrayed him later.

⇨ *Earning goodwill*

We should help people with whatever we can. They will remember us for a long time. Bheema earned a good name in the society with his generosity. This was evident in the number of people who turned up to pay homage when he died. He failed to earn the same with his close relatives.

We need to balance between our public and our private lives.

Self-action Plan

Actions   **By When**

1.

2.

3.

Review after Three Months

People First

A good criterion for measuring success is the number of people you have made happy.

– Robert J Lumsden

For any company, institution or organisation to succeed, according to the Toyota Motors, it needs to concentrate on the 4Ps, namely Product, Process, People and Promotion. Which one is the most important? For long term sustenance, all are important, but the most important is people. They are the foundation of any organisational structure. As a nation, should we focus on people or infrastructure? The choice makes a difference between culture and comfort.

There was a competition at a function. Participants were given parts of a puzzle that they had to put together. The final output was the India map. The one who completed it first would be the winner. An illiterate person won the competition. Everyone was surprised and asked him how he did it. He said that he noticed that on the back of the puzzle, the picture was that of a human body. He assembled it using the picture at the back as reference and got the India map right. The message is clear. To build a nation, people have to be set right.

The Great Wall of China was begun in the 7th century BC by Qin Shi Huang. Over the years, it has been rebuilt and maintained. It is one of the Wonders of the World. The original rulers thought of the Great Wall as a protection from enemies. They thought that no one could climb the wall and that the land would be safe. But in the first 100 years of the wall, the land was invaded thrice. Enemies didn't climb the wall but bribed guards and came through the doors. The rulers focused on the walls but didn't focus on building human character.

In the book, "Good to Great," author Jim Collins suggests that we decide "who" first before "what." If we want to do a project or business, he suggests that, we should decide who should get into our bus and where they should be seated. People who do not align with the objective of the business are to be asked to get down from the bus. With the right people in the bus, we can decide on where to go.

Character-building should start with family and education. Good parents and teachers can build a wonderful nation by building wonderful people. As a society, we should learn to respect their roles. People are not real assets, but the right people are assets, says Jim Collins. India as a country can benefit from the young population only if we focus on building their characters.

Are we ready?

Self-action Plan

Actions	By When

1.

2.

3.

Review after Three Months

Response versus Reaction

The greatest mistake we humans make in our relationships is that we listen half, understand quarter, think zero and react double.

– Anonymous

In a company where I support, I noticed that they were using too many CFL bulbs in a particular hangar. Considering the savings of running cost and contribution to environment, I wrote a mail to the Plant Manager to consider LED in place of CFL bulbs. I also suggested the name of an LED manufacturer who could be called to evaluate the Return on Investment. He replied saying that they were replacing the CFL bulbs with the LED when they were not working or burnt out. I found out from others that they had bought a few CFL bulbs very recently. I wrote back saying that replacing the bulbs one by one will not work well in LED, from my experience. Changing to LED on the shop floor would also mean changing the fittings. It would take years to replace all, if done one by one. Another reply came quickly, telling me that LED bulb installations need heavy investment and considering the financial position of the company, the LED option will be considered later. Of course, there were no specific timelines for review or on exact next steps.

If we look closely at the above incident, the Plant Manager just reacted to a situation. He just wanted to close the discussion without really evaluating the idea or the purpose behind it. He could have waited for the evaluation of ROI from the LED manufacturer, then taken a decision based on viability. He chose not to do it.

The family had just purchased a brand new car. That evening, the watchman informed the father that his son had scribbled something on the car. Angry, the father slapped the son. He went to see the damage and found that the son had written, "I love you daddy" with a piece of chalk on the car. It just had to be wiped off and had caused no real damage to the car. The father repented his act but the damage was done. The father reacted here, instead of responding.

A politician, a monk and a servant had to stay overnight in a dense forest. At midnight, they could hear the howling of foxes. The servant ignored the sounds and went to sleep. The monk aligned his mind to tune in to the howling and soon, he began to enjoy the sounds. The politician was worried and afraid whether the fox would attack him. He was very disturbed and could not sleep.

We can see how each one responded to the same situation. How each of us responds therefore, comes from our mental make-up.

We react to phone calls, mails or a letter immediately without thinking. To respond, would mean deeper thought, with an effort to understand, evaluate options and then reply. Reactions sometimes give a negative impression; therefore, response would be better. Reactions can spoil a relationship with a customer or the other person seeking the input. We have the choice to think and respond, so that outcomes are positive.

What should our choice be?

Self-action Plan

Actions	By When
1.	
2.	
3.	

Review after Three Months

How Much Money We Need?

Wealth consists not in having great possessions, but in having few wants.

– Epictetus

On the surface, the above question may seem stupid. You may ask, how can there be a limit on the money we need? Agreed. There is nothing wrong in aspiring to earn more money. But it should be earned in a legitimate way and it should not be accumulated but spent for a good cause. In a lecture by a Swamiji, I heard that there are five things that we can pray for every day for happy living. They are – enough prosperity, long life, good health, peace of mind and wisdom. Notice here the word "enough prosperity." Craving for money accumulation creates stress through the fear of loss, selfishness and mistrust.

Let me illustrate with a story from the Panchatantra. Deva Sharma was an intelligent man. People used to go to him with their problems for his advice. They used to pay him for his efforts. Slowly, he accumulated a lot of money.

At the end of the day, he would count all his monies and think about how to add more. The money or assets he accumulated were in the form of gold coins. He would carry all the gold coins in a bundle whenever he went. He was afraid of losing it.

A cheat, Ashadabhoothi, decided to snatch the bag of gold coins from Deva Sharma. He approached him on the pretext of learning the Shiva Mantra from him. Deva Sharma agreed to take him on as a disciple and allowed him to stay with him. Ashadabhoothi acted very submissive. Ashadabhoothi soon won the goodwill of the guru.

They were travelling together once. They reached a river and Deva Sharma wanted to take a bath. He told his disciple to take care of the treasure while he bathed. The thief was waiting for just this opportunity to loot the money. He robbed not just the treasure but also the trust of the guru.

There are many people like Deva Sharma. Many a time, we struggle to accumulate wealth, only to have it snatched cunningly by someone.

So let us be sensible about money and decide how much to earn and use.

Self-action Plan

Actions   **By When**

1.

2.

3.

Review after Three Months

Taking Control of Ourselves

My life didn't please me, so I created my life.

– Coco Chanel

Who is the best person to help us? The right answer is ourselves. Nothing happens without our permission. We cannot blame someone else for where we are or our situation in life. We must take control 100% of our life. Only then will life be the way we want. We can take suggestions from others, but the final decision should be taken by us.

Ramu and Anitha were colleagues. During lunch time, they used to eat together. Ramu often complained while opening his lunch box, "It is same old idly (steamed rice cake). I really hate it." Anitha would share her lunch with Ramu. The next day, Ramu said during lunch time, "Again, the same idly. I cannot bear it."

One day Anitha asked, "If you do not like idly why don't you tell your wife to pack something else?" Ramu replied coolly, "I am not married. I cook and pack my box myself."

We are like Ramu many a time. I have heard employees talk about fire-fighting in companies. This refers to last minute dealing of issues. If we analyse the reasons why, we may have created the situation ourselves. We create the fire on one side, and fire fight on the other.

A senior manager in a company passed away. The HR put up a notice about his funeral on the notice board. Many of those who read the notice pretended to be sad outwardly, but were not unhappy at his demise – he had blocked the promotions of many.

They were curious to see who that person was. Each employee in turn, at the burial ground, was allowed to look into the coffin. What they saw was their own face. A mirror had been placed at the bottom of the coffin, so each saw their own reflection. They got the answer to the question as to who really blocked their promotion.

The road block for our own growth and progress is our own thinking, behaviour and attitude. Instead of blaming our parents, spouse, boss, employer and fate, let us take control of our life to create the path we want. The limitations are set by ourselves.

No one stops us without our permission. Which area of life can we take control of?

Self-action Plan

Actions   **By When**

1.

2.

3.

Review after Three Months

Missed Opportunity

Opportunities are like sunrises. If you wait too long, you miss them.

– William Arthur Ward

It is said that success does not come if we are not prepared when the opportunity arrives. Financial advisers always recommend that we keep some money in reserve to strike when the market situation is favourable. Many times, we miss the opportunity because we are not prepared. Opportunities do come to us, but often, we give reasons why we cannot take them while the actual reason is that we are unprepared.

Let me share something that happened to me. It was 1991. It was my first trip to Europe. I was returning to India from Germany by a Swiss Air flight. At that time, there was no Lufthansa flight to India and other flight options were limited. The Swiss Air hub was in Zurich, Switzerland. I had to wait for about four hours in the airport for the connecting flight to India. I was finding ways to spend this waiting time. I picked up a conversation with an Indian who was also waiting for the same flight. A typical first question was, "Are you also heading to Bangalore?" When he said yes, we began to converse further. During the discussion, I noticed that he had a thick passport with 2–3 old ones stapled together. This was because of the many visa stampings in it. I surmised that he was a frequent traveller and I was curious to know what exactly he did. He said that he was into the software business and also mentioned that he was sick of travelling to Europe so often. His fatigue was because of long haul flights with long waiting periods, rather than time spent in the business itself. He also told me that there were good opportunities coming up in Europe. He revealed that his name was Narayana Murthy and that he had started a company called Infosys a few years back.

Then I remembered that a manager from Bosch (MICO at that time) where I was working at that time, a lady, had joined him as HR head. He said that he had recruited her recently. While we were about to board the flight, he told me to see him at his office in Koramangala (an area in Bangalore, a hub of software start-ups) and that there could be some opportunities to discuss. I knew the location. I said yes and thanked him.

After my return, I got busy with various things and also told my colleagues about my meeting. Their first reaction was that I should not think of joining a start-up, leaving a multinational like Bosch. I may lose all the perks of an established set-up. I found their suggestions validated my resistance to change from a comfort situation. I dropped the idea of meeting Mr. Narayana Murthy and life went on.

I have no regrets that I missed an opportunity to join Infosys. But I could have explored the opportunity certainly. I could have at least met Mr. Narayana Murthy to see what he had in mind for me. When I reflect, I realised that I was not prepared to leave my current job and let go of my comfort zone.

We need not take every opportunity that comes our way. However, keeping our goals in mind, we can be prepared to hit the opportunity we want to, when it strikes.

Are we prepared to take it on?

Self-action Plan

Actions	By When
1.	
2.	
3.	

Review after Three Months

The Power of Passion

The biggest mistake people make in life is not trying to make a living at doing what they most enjoy.

– Molcolm Forbes

If we study the life history of any successful person, what we will notice is their passion for something. That passion drives them to do something meaningful. Passion is nothing but a strong inclination towards something with an emotional drive. Passion will make life more purposeful. By being engaged in something that a person is passionate about, he or she will put in a hundred percent. They also get pleasure in engaging this way.

We all know Pandit Jasraj, the well-known Hindustani singer. In an interview, a journalist asked him about his deep involvement and dedication to music. The Pandit replied that, fortunately for him, his passion and profession were same. He is so successful because he is doing what he likes the most.

Look at the story of the founder of the most famous sports shoe brand, Nike. His name is William Jay Bowerman. In America, at the start of his career, he was a biology teacher and was interested in football. He wanted to be a football coach rather than a player. He was coaching as well as teaching biology. He later became head track coach at the University of Oregon. His passion for coaching was so much that he started looking at innovative ways of playing the game, as well as unique ways of warming up with jogging.

He found that the type and quality of shoes worn by sportsmen played an important role in the game. He thought of a light shoe which would be stylish, durable and comfortable. He co-founded the Nike shoe company and was head of design for the company. He dedicated his life to creating the right shoes that helped sportsmen, especially athletes, to perform better in the field. Now it is history and Nike is the first name globally for anyone looking for a sports shoe. This would not have happened without the founder's passion to make better shoes for sportsmen.

When a journalist asked Isaac Asimov, the Russian writer who wrote 500 books, what he would like to be remembered as – a wonderful writer, a world-famous author, a great philosopher, Asimov said that he would like to be remembered as someone who enjoyed writing all his life. That is passion. It is doing things for oneself and not for recognition. I do not think he would have written so many books if he had focused on just fame.

Many who want to be entrepreneurs start looking for domains which are lucrative and economically rewarding. Economic considerations are definitely a factor to consider, but more important, is to focus on where one's passion lies.

The person who is passionate about teaching and training, should get into a teaching or training job.

I recently addressed the teachers of an engineering college. I discovered that many of them were not passionate about interacting with students or teaching. They had joined the college for a job. The college had also not bothered to check this aspect at the time of recruitment. The result was evident when looking at the section of de-motivated staff and students.

Shall we start looking inward to check what exactly our passion is?

Self-action Plan

Actions	By When
1.	
2.	
3.	

Review after Three Months

Words Can Be a Sword

Words are like eggs dropped from great heights. You can no more call them back than ignore the mess they leave when they fall.

– Jodi Picoult

Whether orally or in writing, words have a great impact. If not used properly, they can act like a sword. If WORDS are rearranged, SWORD emerges. Words once uttered, cannot be taken back. Our relationship with others depends on the type of words we use.

Ram was a brilliant student. He was doing well in his studies. His parents' expectations were high. They wanted Ram to do something which they could not do in their life. Their wish was that Ram become an engineer. They talked about this with everyone they knew. To achieve their wish, Mother used to tell Ram every day, "What you are doing is not enough," "Look at my friend's son. How hard he is studying," "Given a chance, you spend lot of time with the TV and mobile without studying," "I do not think you will become an engineer with such efforts," "Why don't you learn from your cousin?," "At least you should become an engineer in our family," and so on. These words, heard almost daily, conditioned Ram's mind. It made him think that what he was doing was not enough, that he was inferior to others and that he could not become an engineer. His fear increased with the pressure of the upcoming examinations and expectations of parents. He did not do well in the final examinations. As a result, he became dejected and got into other habits. His parents wounded him further with more piercing words. Words spoiled the life of a boy.

There was a monkey on a tree near a river. From the top of the tree, it saw a fish in the water. The kind-hearted monkey felt miserable to see the fish drowning. It jumped into the water to save the fish. The monkey felt happy when it pulled the fish out, thinking it had saved the life of the fish. The intention of monkey was good, but the act was bad. Can we draw a parallel to the act Ram's parents? Their intention to see their son succeed was good. But their approach was not correct. They thought words would motivate Ram. But what happened was different.

Using the right words while talking is an art. When we learn to speak well, we can rise high in life. Personalities like Vivekananda, Gandhiji, Ramakrishna Paramahamsa, Abdul Kalam and others are examples of this. The words we use reflect our image and attract or distance people. We can influence others by talking properly, using the right words. People understand us only by our words. Words have the power. People do not remember our words. But they remember the impact the words made on them.

Thank you for reading these words. Which kind of words do you want to use?

Self-action Plan

Actions   **By When**

1.

2.

3.

Review after Three Months

The Gift Called Present

Exhale the past without any regret, inhale the future without any expectation and hold the present with pleasure.

– Anonymous

So much has been written about time management. Actually, it is a misnomer since we cannot manage a commodity which cannot be increased or decreased. We can only change our priorities to make the best use of time. The problem with using the available time now is that our mind is occupied with the memories of the past and anxieties of the future, leaving us little time to be in the present. To understand the value of microseconds, we should ask an Olympic athlete. Each second lost cannot be regained even if we are ready to pay gold for it.

Swami Chinmayananda, founder of the well-known Chinmaya Mission, was once asked by a disciple just before a lecture he was to give, as to how the Swamiji was so energetic always. The disciple knew about his busy schedule and about his health condition. The Swamiji replied, "What happened yesterday or the day before does not bother me. I am not concerned about the future as I do not know what it will bring. I engage myself 100% in the present." The Swamiji conserved his energy to spend it in the present and was therefore energetic.

Of the past, present and future, the most important is the present. We have no control over the past. Can we drive a car looking only at the rear mirror? No way. But the rear view gives us some indications of how we are to correct ourselves as we move forward. We cannot bring back the past. For every regret, put in an expiry date.

The future is unknown to all of us. Why be concerned about it, imagining problems? The only choice left for us to live fully in the present, making effective use of time. If we do not make use of the opportunities available to us now, it will soon become past, and we may have to just regret. The past is demonetised currency, the future is a promissory note; and the present is the cash. Let us make good use of it now. Rivers never flow in the reverse direction. Be like a river and keep flowing forward, forgetting the past.

There was a businessman who was always busy earning money. He considered that spending time with his wife and children was a waste of time. That time could be used better in business. Because of overwork without any relaxation, he got a heart attack. By that time, he was already 60 years old. The doctor who treated him advised him rest and that he spend some time with the family.

With this wake-up call, he started thinking how he had wasted years not spending time with the family. He had always been thinking of how to make money for the future. He now decided to live in the present. He guessed that he would die at the age of 80. So he had 20 more years to go. He brought 1,040 marble round pebbles and put them in a glass jar. He kept the jar in the hall. 1,040 were actual weeks left for him in this world. He wanted to make use them fully. Each weekend, he would spend time fully with the family and throw out one pebble. The reducing number of pebbles reminded him of how life was eroding. He had to make the best use of time available now.

God's best gift for us is the present. Lao Tsu said, "If you are depressed you are living in the past; if you are anxious you are living in the future and if you are at peace, you live in the present."

Incidentally, GIFT and PRESENT have the same meaning. Let us use this gift fully.

Self-action Plan

Actions   **By When**

1.

2.

3.

Review after Three Months

Be Open-Minded

There is a saying in the Rig Veda, "Let noble thoughts come to us from every side." But noble thoughts can come only if we are open-minded to accept them. A closed mind cannot accept any new ideas for improvement. The reason for having a closed mind could be because of past incidents, arrogance or an "I-know-it-all" attitude. Prejudice or pre-conceived notions can also be a reason.

An atheist once asked the Buddha, "I don't think there is a God. Do you believe in GOD?" Buddha said, "No." Then a theist asked the Buddha, "I strongly believe that there is God. Do you believe in God?" The Buddha said, "Yes." As he walked further, he met another person who asked him, "I do not know whether God is there or not. Will you help me find out?" The Buddha said, "Let us explore together." Later one of his disciples asked the Buddha why he gave different answers to the atheist and the theist. The Buddha replied, "They have already formed their opinion and only wanted an answer to validate theirs. But the third person was open-minded and curious. Only open-minded people can learn."

We cannot change a person who is not willing to change. His or her close-minded thinking will not allow him to listen to us. Instead of wasting time with such people it is better to let go.

Recently, I did a corporate training where participants were from the senior management. Their mindset was that, with the long years of their experience, what could a trainer teach them? They had literally closed their minds to listen to any new thinking. I could break their mindset only when I explained how each year of experience acts as an insulation layer on them, which makes it difficult for any new knowledge to penetrate. They began to appreciate my session better when they realised the benefits of unlearning and relearning.

The mind is like a parachute. It works best when it is open. Close-minded people miss many opportunities because of their resistance to accept new ideas. A person with an open mind will typically not judge others, be open to others' opinions, respect others' beliefs, will try new things, be inquisitive enough to learn new domains, be ready to accept changes and accept responsibilities. Acharya Rajneesh preached, that we have to see this world daily as if we are seeing it for the first time, with an open mind. He said that the secret of living in the present is to enjoy every moment.

Even if we know something, let us take inputs from others with an open mind, to see further possibilities for improvement.

Self-action Plan

Actions   **By When**

1.

2.

3.

Review after Three Months

Carrying Baggage
in the Mind

I have decided to stick to love. Hate is too great a burden to bear.
– Martin Luther King Jr

Many of us are jealous of someone who is better than us or worth more than us. It slowly develops into a sort of hatred for them. We also develop a hatred for those who made us angry some time or the other. We are reluctant to forgive them. There is a beautiful saying, "If someone likes you, you are in their heart. If they do not like you, you are still in their mind. Either way, they remember you – be happy about it."

The teacher asked her students to bring fresh apples to the school next day with a sticker on each. The sticker will have the name of the person the student hates. They were to bring one apple for each person hated. The students brought the apples. The number of apples varied for each student. Some had just two, some had five, ten and some brought even upto 20 numbers. The teacher instructed the students to carry the bag of apples for the next two weeks wherever they went.

As the days passed, the students complained about the bad smell of the apples as they began to spoil. Those who carried larger numbers complained about the additional weight they had to carry along with foul smell. Finally, the teacher asked the students to throw away all the spoilt apples. The teacher said, "We carry with us in our minds, hatred for people. It is a burden for us. Is it not additional baggage? How light we would have been without this burden! Also, the foul smell spoils our mind as well. It makes our thinking unhealthy. So, like we did the spoilt apples, we should throw away the hatred. The mind is like a garden and should be cleaned regularly. Forgive those who have angered you. Get better and not bitter."

The Buddha said that carrying jealousy or hatred is like carrying fire. It will only burn us and not the other person. To ignite our mind, we should make it dry and free from wetness of hatred, jealousy, anger and ego.

Shall we begin to cleanse our minds?

Self-action Plan

Actions	By When
1.	
2.	
3.	

Review after Three Months

Never Give Up

One of the common causes of failure is the habit of quitting when one is overtaken by temporary defeat.

– Napolean Hill

In whatever we do, there will be some issues to deal with. In fact, it would be a surprise if there were no issues. When everything is alright, something may be wrong. It's better to look at whether we are on the right path. I like what Michael Jordan said once: "If you are trying to achieve something... there will be road blocks. I have had them, everybody has had them. But obstacles don't have to stop you. If you run into a wall, don't turn around and give up. Figure out how to climb it, go through it or work around it." Giving up at the first encounter of an obstacle is a losing proposition.

In a marketing job, to find new customers, contacts have to be made. The marketing person will be very enthusiastic about the contacts in the beginning but would give up after sometime. As per the study done by Herbert True, Notre Dame University, 44% of all sales people quit trying after the first call, 24% quit after the second call, 14% quit after the third call, 12% quit trying after the fourth call. That means, 94% of sales people quit after the fourth call. He also showed from his study that 60% of sales are made after the fourth call. For a marketing person, 'NO' means 'Next Opportunity.' Without bothering much about these numbers, we can fairly confidently say that by not giving up, the chances of success are better. Vince Lombardi, the famous American football coach said, "A Quitter never wins and a Winner never quits."

J K Rowling, the author of the Harry Potter series faced endless rejections by publishers. The typical reasons were, "Children's books never make any money," "It is too long for children," etc. But she never gave up. Now 400+ million copies of Harry Potter books are being sold.

Henry Ford, one of the founders of the automobile revolution, had many failures on his way. His first initiative to build a motor car fell apart in a year and a half as its stockholders lost confidence in Henry Ford. Ford gathered capital to start again, but because of pressure from financiers, he had to stop. Though everyone in the industry had lost hope in him, he managed to find another investor to start the Ford Motor Company. The rest is now history.

The reasons for giving up could be lack of confidence, waiting endlessly for the ideal situation, inability to handle feedback and lack of focus or a clear target. People leave when there is ambiguity in what they do. Swami Vivekananda said, "Take up one idea. Make that one idea your life – think of it, dream of it, live on that idea. Let the brain, muscles, nerves, every part of your body, be full of that idea and just leave every other idea alone. This is the way of success, and this is the way great spiritual giants are produced."

We shall strive not to quit whatever we take up.

Self-action Plan

Actions   **By When**

1.

2.

3.

Review after Three Months

Leaving a Legacy

Someone can sit in the shade today because someone planted a tree long time ago.

– Warren Buffet

"Legacy" as per the dictionary definition, means "leaving for the next generation our inheritance, properties and whatever material acquisitions." It could be in the form of a will. Our life will be meaningful if we leave for the next generations, our thoughts, principles and values. The good things we acquire over the years through struggle, should not lapse with us. The next generation should benefit from our knowledge and wisdom. In Jewish tradition, 'Ethical Wills' are written where they pass on to the next generation, the gift of wisdom and good wishes. It conveys values, hopes and conviction. This is far more profound than bequests of property.

We see many old trees planted by our forefathers. If they had been selfish, they probably would not have bothered to plant those trees. We are getting the benefits of their selfless legacy. Legacy is not something that comes up after our death, but is to be created when are alive.

Mohandas Karamchand Gandhi struggled through his life to throw British rule out of India. He was greatly influenced by the discrimination he experienced in South Africa. He developed the idea of passive resistance against the authorities and called it Satyagraha. When he returned to India, he fought against the colonial British Government. He encouraged his followers to protest peacefully, fight against inequality, to be self-sufficient, follow the path of truth and to lead simple lives. He followed lifestyle of fasting, prayer and meditation. His commitment to the cause was exemplary. He sacrificed everything to get freedom for India. He left behind a legacy of truth, peace, simplicity and equality. The next generations continued these legacies and even today, many follow his principles. Gandhi is a known name all over the world even after generations.

Generations follow and remember the legacy of people who lived for others. It could be Gandhi, Swami Vivekananda, Nelson Mandela, John F Kennedy, Martin Luther King, Mother Teresa, Sister Nivedita, etc. These men or women sacrificed their lives for the causes for which they lived. Their contributions were so significant that with their death, they have left behind a spectacular legacy. They immortalised the principles they spearheaded. Many of them became martyrs. People like Adolf Hitler, Saddam Hussain, Benito Mussolini, etc. created a legacy of selfishness, hatred and narrow-minded thinking. They are remembered for what they created. Things we do for ourselves will be gone when we are gone. But things done for others remain as our legacy.

Great leaders believe that the purpose of life is to live for others, create new things and to pass on a good legacy to the next generations. John Donne says, "The critical day in our life is not the day of our death but the whole course of our life." Leaving a legacy is not about something that comes after our lives; it is about the way we live. It is about learning from the experience of the past, and living in the present to create a future.

What we do today is the future, because that is what leaves a lasting legacy.

What shall we attempt to leave as legacy?

Self-action Plan

Actions	By When
1.	
2.	
3.	

Review after Three Months

Acts of Compassion

All I ever wanted was to reach out and touch another human being not just with my hands but with my heart.

– Tahereh Mafi

In our childhood, we pick up thoughts and habits which will remain with us forever. One such thing that lingers in my memory is this: I was in high school in my small home town when this incident happened. School was two kilometres by walk, from my home. That walk was the most interesting, despite being between two stressful destinations. One evening, while returning from school, we, a group of boys, saw a person who seemed like he was mad. It was fun for us to mock him and irritate him. The madman had a lot of wounds on his body and was shouting, *"Uppindi, Uppindi"* (the name of a typical Andhra Pradesh dish). He was also murmuring something which we could not understand.

When I reached home, my grandfather was waiting for me. He was known for his high level of discipline and often gave a helping hand to the needy. He said that he had seen our behaviour with the madman and advised us not to do such things. I did not care for his words. That was not all. He asked my mother to prepare *uppittu* (the equivalent of *uppindi* in Kannada). Later, he asked me to take the *uppittu* and give it to the madman. Grandfather also gave me a sort of herbal medicine to apply on his wounds.

The madman was joyous when he saw the *uppindi* in my hand and grabbed and ate it. I applied the medicine on his body with reluctance. I observed that the madman was silent as he was focusing on eating. This exercise went on for the next 3–4 days. The next day, the madman had vanished. He must have gone to his next destination.

Though this incident happened a long time back, it is still in my memory. My grandfather is no more. But the wonderful act of compassion that I learnt in my childhood through grandfather guides me even now.

In what way can we be compassionate to the less fortunate?

Self-action Plan

Actions	By When
1.	
2.	
3.	

Review after Three Months

To Be Selectively Deaf

I was deaf, dumb and blind to all but me, myself and I.

– Loretta Young

I am sure all of us have been in a situation where we wanted to do something and someone made a remark which discouraged us from doing so. In the corporate world, good ideas have been killed by a few killer phrases. A few examples of these phrases are, "We cannot do this. Too difficult," "It does not work in India," "If it is so simple, why has no one done it so far," "We tried this long back and it didn't work," "I do not think that the customer will approve of this" and so on.

Many ideas are killed before they are born. Every day, many negative words keep on falling on our ears, discouraging our attempts to do something. For example, if a child wants to play cricket and has an interest in it, he may hear a remark from his parents, "Why waste time in sports? You cannot become Sachin Tendulkar. Better to do something that can get you a job." Eventually the child may lose interest in its favourite game.

A colony of frogs were living in a pond. They were very comfortable. One hot summer the water in the pond began to dry up. It became difficult to survive day by day. They all decided to move to another pond next to a mountain nearby. To go to that pond, they had to cross the mountain. It was a rough terrain.

One morning, all the frogs decided to move to the new pond. As the sun came up, the frogs became very tired. Some frogs decided to return saying they could not cross the mountain. Seeing this, others too felt discouraged. Soon, the entire colony returned to the old pond. Only one frog kept hopping towards the mountain. Others shouted at this frog, "Hey, enough. We will go back. You cannot climb the mountain." But the frog never looked back. He kept hopping. When it reached the top of the mountain, it looked back and shouted at other frogs below, "I cannot hear anything you say. I am born deaf. Start moving to the top!" Because the frog was deaf, it could not hear the negative and discouraging words of others.

We should keep moving towards our goal without listening to discouraging remarks, gossip and negative words. We need to be deaf even for our internal voice in our head that throws up negative thoughts, fear, uncertainty, ambiguity and confusion.

Better to be deaf sometimes!

Self-action Plan

Actions	**By When**
1.	
2.	
3.	

Review after Three Months

Process versus Result Approach

Every problem has a solution, but they may not be your choice. Do your best to solve the problem and accept the solution that comes out.

– Eknath Ranade

There is always a debate if the focus has to be on the process or the result. One argument is that result is important as that is the only purpose for doing anything, so how does the process matter? The second argument says that process is important since only good processes will lead to good results. The Americans, it is said, focus on the results, while the Japanese focus on process. Toyota, a Japanese company, has given the acronyms MBR (Management by Result) and MBM (Management by Means) for these two approaches.

There was an automobile company manufacturing bikes. The new CEO of the company was aggressive in wanting to increase sales to reach a certain market share. As expected, the target went to the sales department. It percolated to each of the sales executives. To motivate them to sell more, the company offered an incentive package if they reached targets. The sales force started aggressive marketing. Keeping the incentive in mind, their focus was somehow only on selling the bikes. They knew very well that the vehicle had many problems but they concealed these from the prospective buyers. The sales force was not worried about the implication of the wrong sales process, and were not hesitant to tell lies to achieve their objective of selling. They achieved their targets and got their incentives.

The CEO also got credit for increasing the market share. What happened later? Customers who bought the bikes experienced issues and were not happy about the false information given at the time of selling. They felt cheated. They in turn, spread information about the poor quality of the bike to friends. The bike soon got negative reviews and sales plummeted.

Instead of the result approach in selling, if the CEO had called the sales force to tell them openly about the features of the bike and had taken inputs from them on the improvements needed based on customer feedback, the sales numbers would have been less, but customer-loyalty would have been ensured. This process approach would have helped the company survive longer.

The result approach is for the shorter term. For long term sustenance, the process approach is better. After establishing the process, the focus should be on how to make the process robust and reliable.

Which approach suits you?

Self-action Plan

Actions   **By When**

1.

2.

3.

Review after Three Months

Taking Help from Others

No man will make a Leader who wants to do it all by himself or get all the credit for doing it.

– Ingrid Bergman

Many times, we are hesitant to ask others for help. The reason could be because of our ego, shyness, fear that others may think badly of us or a feeling that I know best. We should remember that we cannot be experts in everything and should seek help from others without hesitation. It will not make us inferior. Seeking help builds relationships and develops interdependency.

I was struggling to locate a source for a specific product and wasted a lot of time in searching for it. Suddenly, it occurred to me to seek the help of friends. Things became easy after that as most of my friends were happy to help. In this process, we should not forget to thank them. When the opportunity comes, we should also repay such help.

I have observed that many in the younger generation seem to have the attitude of I-know-it-all and are hesitant to ask for help. Recently, I gave an assignment to a student for a part of a master's degree requirement. I offered him any help needed for proper understanding before writing the assignment. He never did ask me and in the submission, I found that he had understood fundamentals wrongly and had written irrelevant information. I asked him why he had not asked for my help. His reply was, "Sir, I assumed that you would think less of me if I ask for help."

A young girl and her father were walking down a forest path. A large tree branch had fallen across their path and was blocking their way. The girl asked her father, "Do you think I could move the branch?" Her father replied, "I am sure you can, if you use all your strength."

The girl tried her best to lift or push the branch, but in vain. She said, "You were wrong, dad. I can't move it." "Try again with all your strength," replied her father. The girl tried again, but in vain. She gave up. Her father said, "Young lady, I advised you to use all your strength. You didn't. You didn't ask for my help."

Our strength is not in independence but in interdependence. Asking others for help is not a sign of weakness, but of wisdom.

Will you help me?

Self-action Plan

Actions   **By When**

1.

2.

3.

Review after Three Months

Orientation to Work

Ability is what you are capable of doing. Motivation determines what you do. Attitude determines how well you do it.

– Anonymous

Our attitude towards the task we are doing has a great influence on the outcome. If we feel proud about the work we are doing, we are satisfied and fulfilled. Stress from work will get eliminated. Someone asked a mother why she does not get bored cooking for their family every day. She said that she considers the task a sacred job and feels good when she sees her family happy and healthy.

A traveller came across three stone cutters. He asked them what they were doing. The first one said that he was cutting stones. The second stone cutter said that he was making a step from the stone and was bringing a shape to the rock. The third stone cutter said proudly that he was helping build a temple.

Though all three stone cutters were doing the same job, their orientation and outlook towards their job was different. Similarly, in any organisation, the outlook of the employee and the feeling of pride in his or her job, is very vital for the growth of the organisation. While being engaged in work, one must not forget the focus on the 'temple' as in the stone cutter story. It does not matter what job we do, but our orientation towards it decides our involvement in the job. If a software engineer feels that he is not just fulfilling the expectations of his employer but helping society productively by enriching knowledge, his contribution to the organisation will go beyond what is expected of him.

In one company that I often visited, a lady's job profile was to bend a wire. She had been doing it for many years, to my knowledge. However, she had no idea of the importance of her job. One day, I spoke to her and told her where her job fitted in the manufacturing process and in the product and how important it was. She understood the need for her to take care to do a good job. She felt proud about her work as well.

Irrespective of the job we do, we need to see the bigger picture and orient ourselves accordingly.

How is our orientation?

Self-action Plan

Actions   **By When**

1.

2.

3.

Review after Three Months

Sharpening the Axe

Give me six hours to chop down a tree and I will spend the first four hour sharpening the axe.

– Abraham Lincoln

What we learnt few years ago, may not be valid today. The world is changing continuously and we need to upgrade ourselves suitably. But what happens is, our old learnings fill us so completely that they leave us with hardly any room for new learnings. We need to focus on unlearning to remove some old practices and thinking, to replace these suitably with new skills. It is like a bottle with full of water. To improve the quality of water, we need to pour out some water from the bottle to replace with the better water. When we buy a mobile phone or a computer, we always look for the latest software. As time passes, we focus on replacing the old software with the latest versions. Let us ask ourselves, how often we upgrade the software in our mind. Old thinking cannot bring new results. We have to upgrade ourselves continuously. It is like the sharpening of an axe by a woodcutter so that he is able to cut the wood effectively.

Two woodcutters were friends. One was very thin and weak. The other was fat and strong. They used to go to the forest every day to cut trees. One day, the weak woodcutter cut 15 trees, while the strong one cut 18 trees. He was filled with pride comparing himself to his weak friend. The next day, both of them could cut only 15 trees. As the days passed, the weak man continued to cut 15 trees every day; however, the strong one's output reduced to ten trees.

What went wrong? Every day in the evening after work, while the strong woodcutter was sleeping filled with the pride of his strength, the weak woodcutter was sharpening his axe. He was able to cut a consistent number of trees every day.

Are we spending time learning new skills and new ways of doing things? Are we allocating time for learning?

Let us identify the learning gap – let us sharpen our axes to enable us to do more things effectively.

Self-action Plan

Actions	By When
1.	
2.	
3.	

Review after Three Months

The Art of Adjustment

The life will not adjust to us. We need to find ways to adjust ourselves to life.

– Anonymous

The need for adjustment is one of the biggest lessons of life. We cannot change others, but by adjusting, we can make the change. I am not referring adjustment in the negative sense for any selfish gain. Adjustment is a must in office, in personal life and in society. Even parents should learn to adjust themselves to children, especially when they grow up. Children must also learn to adjust with ageing parents. To do this, we may have to shed our ego. Adjustment is a sort of sacrifice and could also mean some compromise. But we should not adjust our values, ethics and our philosophy. Adjustment is a sort of middle path taken by both the parties involved for a win-win situation.

Lalitha could not adjust to living with her mother-in-law as their personalities were different. Every day, they would argue and fight for some silly reason. Lalitha's husband was a spectator and was in distress. When things became unbearable, Lalitha decided to find a solution. She met an old teacher, explained her problem and sought a poison in the form of a medicine to kill her mother-in-law. The teacher specialised in preparing various herbs to treat diseases. The teacher gave her some herbs and told her to give a small dose of it with milk every day, to her mother-in-law. She would then die slowly and no one would suspect Lalitha. She also had to pretend to love her mother-in-law. Lalitha started the treatment.

Over a period of time, the mother-in-law noticed the change in her daughter-in-law and she in turn, started treating her well. The situation improved and both started adjusting to each other.

The daughter-in-law felt guilty now, returned to the teacher and said, "Teacher, my mother-in-law is a very nice lady. We have adjusted to each other well. I do not want her to die. Please give me herbs to reverse the poison." The teacher smiled and said that the herbs were just vitamins and were not poison. The poison was in the minds of both the ladies.

Lack of adjustment sometimes takes a toll on our health, energy, position and wealth. Developing interrelationships with adjustment can make life beautiful. Lack of adjustment is one reason why there are so many divorces.

"Let us agree to disagree," is a popular phrase. Let us learn to give and take, and adjust that little bit to make life sweeter.

Self-action Plan

Actions   **By When**

1.

2.

3.

Review after Three Months

Falling Is Not a Failure

Every adversity, every failure, every heartache carries with it seed of an equal or greater benefit.

– Napolean

I met a school classmate after nearly 40 years. It was in the same small town where we had done our schooling together. It had been a village in our growing years; now it was a small town. Our chats started with old memories of how we teased our teachers, got beaten up; how we were afraid to talk to girls and how we fought over a biscuit packet distributed at a school function. In between, we munched on endless eatables served by the family members. My friend, for some reason, did not have a college education. He is a freelance priest in a village near our hometown. However, we never allowed our changed social status to come in between our friendship. Compare this to the many so-called business friends. Let me park this point here and move further with the story.

Having met as a family after decades, we decided to go on a picnic together. This would give us more time to interact with each other and to explore the old places where we had played in childhood. When I suggested that we walk 3 km to reach the picnic spot, he demurred. He wanted to drive the long route, 15 kms. When I asked him why, he told me that he had once walked the 3 km stretch about 10 years ago, fallen on the slippery stretch and had broken an arm. He did not want to risk it again.

I told him that things may have changed. Could we try to walk the short route again? We were in for a pleasant surprise. The short route had been developed as a walking path, and it was now easily navigable, He was surprised to and we enjoyed the walk.

We all do react like my friend did. We retain memories of a bad experience and do not try to do it again. We remember the fall or the failure. We do not think that situations or circumstances could change.

Let us not be afraid of failing. Thinking of failure or of making a mistake, we may not attempt to do a thing. Perfectionists hate failure and create stress for themselves in the process. Remember the words of Confucius, "Better be a diamond with a flaw than a pebble without." Failure means that we are attempting to move out of our comfort zones and is an indication that we are growing. With failure comes better insight, which can be applied to improvements. The world is here today because of trial and error, failure and success. Let us look back at our failures with pride and understand the role they played in our growth. Jack Canfield said, "Don't worry about failures. Worry about the chances you miss when you don't even try."

As someone rightly said, "Falling is not failure. But failing to get up is failure." Failure may be a bend in life but not the end.

Are we ready to move further, not worrying about failure?

Self-action Plan

    Actions   **By When**

1.

2.

3.

Review after Three Months

Weakness Can Be Strength

Every weakness contains within itself a strength.

– Shusaku Endo

We are all born with strengths and weaknesses. Instead of grumbling about the weaknesses that we inherit, and that cannot be changed, we can change our view of looking at it. In the Indian cricket team, there was a world class spinner – Chandrashekhar. His arm had been twisted because of polio, but this helped him become a world class spinning bowler.

The disciple of a Zen guru would carry water daily to the top of hill where his Master sat in mediation. This he did in two earthen pots hung across his shoulder with a stick and ropes. One of the pots had a hole in it and by the time disciple reached the top of the hill, most of the water would have drained from it. This pot felt very bad and felt dejected for its inability to serve its Master properly. It also started comparing itself with the other pot which was always full.

The pot told the Master how it felt one day. The Master replied, "Hey Pot! Have you seen the path on your side? Because water leaks from you, the side where my disciple carries you is beautiful with flowering plants. You have been giving these plants water every day. You are blessed. Do not worry about your defect, which is actually your strength. You are in no away inferior to the other pot. Feel proud that you are able to contribute to helping the flowers bloom."

Every weakness has a positive side. It all depends on how we see it and how we use it. Sometimes, we feel that we have certain weaknesses and blame God, parents, circumstances, teachers or our Fate for it. But our weakness can become our strength one day. It also does not mean that we should develop weaknesses.

Each of us is special and important. The razor blade is sharp, but cannot cut a tree, just as the axe can't cut hair. Everyone is important.

Recognise your weakness and make it your strength.

Self-action Plan

Actions	By When
1.	
2.	
3.	

Review after Three Months

The Law of Karma

How people treat you is their karma. How you react is yours.

– Wayne Dyer

Karma means action. We cannot stop being engaged in action even if we are not doing anything. Our internal organs are in action till the end. Every external action undertaken has a reaction at some point of time. That point could be in a few hours, days, months, years... or can even extend to our next birth. Many times, this reaction that comes up is referred to as destiny. Destiny is created by our actions. If we do good things, the reactions or results will also be good.

Our family was celebrating a function. A policeman arrived to serve a summons to my father to appear in court the next day. This put a stop to the joy of celebrations. We were all stressed and worried. It turned out that my father had signed as a witness in a bank for a loan for one of his friends about five years ago. The friend had not cleared the loan and the bank had gone to court to recover the loan. Now the court wanted the witness to give a statement. My father's action of a few years ago was affecting us now, at the time of celebration.

A man suffered a cardiac arrest. He blamed his fate, his family and the situation he was in. The doctor however did a reality check. The cardiac arrest had happened because of his own lifestyle, where he never ate on time, drank too much alcohol, had no exercise and was stressed most of the time. He had already had a mild heart attack a few years ago. All his accumulated actions had resulted in his health problem. Can he blame destiny when he himself has created it?

Good things will result by engaging in positive actions. How do we know whether we are engaging in good or bad actions? The best teacher is our conscience. Our inner voice is a very good navigator and gives us direction. Many times, we overlook the inner voice.

A man went to the temple every day, praying to God that he would win a lottery. He wanted to be rich overnight. One day God told him, "Devotee, I appreciate your prayer. But please first buy a lottery ticket."

As it is rightly said in the *Bhagavad Gita*, we have control over our actions, but not over the results. But this does not mean that we should do actions blindly. When we are conscious of what the reaction could be, we can make an attempt to change our actions. Whether the result is good or bad depends on the actions. This is the law of karma.

Shall we act positively to create our destiny?

Self-action Plan

Actions   **By When**

1.

2.

3.

Review after Three Months

What Is Important for Us?

Remembering that I will be dead soon is the most important tool I have ever encountered to help me make choices in life. Because almost everything – all external expectations, all pride, all fear of embarrassment or failure – these things just fall away in the face of death, leaving only what is truly important.

– Steve Jobs

Sometimes we go after things which are not important to us. Important here meant those things that help us reach our final goal and which gives us fulfilment and satisfaction. Identification of what is important is the first step for success in life.

A group of rich corporate executives were not happy with their life. They had everything they could aspire for, but always felt that something was missing in life. Money and comforts did not bring them real joy. They decided to meet to discuss how they could be more happy and joyful. They could not find an answer. One of them knew a spiritual teacher and suggested that they meet him.

The group met the teacher. They told him how they had everything in life, yet felt a vacuum. They also experienced a lot of stress. The teacher offered them coffee. He kept of pot of the brew on the table with a whole range of cups, in gold, silver, porcelain, terracotta, etc. He told the group to help themselves.

When everyone had served themselves, the teacher said, "Dear friends, I notice that each one of you have taken most expensive cups you could choose. The steel ones and the terracotta ones are left behind. Each one of you wants the best things that life can offer. However, what is important – the cup or the coffee? Your problem is this. Actually, you wanted a good coffee; instead you focused on the holder of the coffee which has no role in the taste of the coffee. This is what you are doing in life too. You are going after those things which do not bring any taste to your life. To feel contented, stress-free and fulfilled, shift your focus from the cup to the coffee."

This is what happens in our life. Position, money, car and other things are like the cup for the coffee. By focusing on them alone, our quality of life will not change.

Let us identify what is important for us and move on.

Self-action Plan

Actions   **By When**

1.

2.

3.

Review after Three Months

Attitude of Gratitude

Feeling gratitude and not expressing it is like wrapping a present and not giving it.

– William Arthur

All of us have somebody who has helped us directly and indirectly. How many of them do we remember? To them do we express our gratitude? By expressing thanks for the help received, we instil a joy and sense of fulfilment in them.

I remember a warden from my hostel days who encouraged me to continue my studies in pre-university. I wanted to leave the college because I could not cope up with the English language medium, having studied in Kannada in high school. When I was struggling, he instilled confidence in me, offered to support by bringing me in contact with the right friends and ensured that I would not give up. With that confidence, I did very well in college and got the highest mark in class. I also studied further. Unfortunately, by the time I realised the value of his help, he was no more. I regret today that I did not express my gratitude in time.

There was a lady who sold flowers door-to-door. One day, before handing over the flowers to us, she extended her arm and offered the flowers in these directions – up, down, sideways and towards me. Taken aback, I asked her why. She said, "Sir, yours is the first house today for me. Before I start my selling I am thanking all the people who are helping me." I told her to explain further. "Pointing towards the ground, I am thanking Goddess Earth for giving me these flowers, the upward action is to thank the Rain God, by moving my arm sideways I thank the farmers who have grown these flowers, as well as my husband and children for allowing to my business to flourish – and finally you, the customer, who buys these flowers." I really felt happy about her attitude of gratitude.

Do we thank our parents for taking care of us, our teachers, our mentors, and others who helped us? It is important that we express gratitude in some way.

One of my friends sends me good articles to read every day. So I sent him a book as a "thank you" for his help. The expression of gratitude can be in words, messages, cards, books or gifts. We can also document our gratitude in our dairy or journal.

Let us express gratitude for all those around us – like drivers, helpers, maids and colleagues for the ways in which they help us. Similarly, let us help others not expecting anything in return.

Who do you want to thank now?

Self-action Plan

Actions   **By When**

1.

2.

3.

Review after Three Months

When One Door Closes...

Business opportunities are like buses, there is always another one coming.

– Richard Branson

When we try something and we are not successful, the normal tendency is to feel bad. We do not realise that not getting a thing is also good for us. By developing this attitude, we will never feel bad when we miss an opportunity. Here, it is important that we put in our 100% efforts to be successful.

After the completion of my 10th standard education, my father identified a good opportunity for me. He believed that starting with a vocational course of four years' duration had better prospects than studying further. Through his brother who lived in Bangalore, he got an application from a multinational company and applied for the vocational course. Though I was qualified, I was not selected because I was not from Bangalore. Their logic was that non-local people would find it difficult to make both ends meet with the meagre stipend from the course. My father felt bad and so did I. My studies continued and I did a masters in engineering from the Indian Institute of Technology. It so happened that I joined the same multinational company and became deputy general manager eventually. Had I got the opportunity as Vocational Trainee, I would have struggled for years and my chances of getting to the level I reached would have been very difficult. I thanked God for closing my first door to open the second, better door.

Desperate for a job, a man applied to a software company for the position of cleaner. He did well in the interview and got selected. The HR manager asked for his email id so that he could send the formal appointment letter. The person who had applied for the job did not have an email and was therefore not selected. Sad, he sat in a tea shop next door to have his tea and bun. He observed good demand for the bun. With the meagre money he had, he purchased buns in bulk and distributed them to many petty tea shops and retained a good margin. Slowly he expanded his business and eventually started his own tea shop. Soon he started a bakery and spread across his footprint across many areas of the city. To insure all his property, he approached an agent and the agent asked for his email to send the prospectus. The man still does not have an email! He told the agent the story of how not having an email saved him from his first job. If he had a mail id, he would have been a cleaner.

We need to believe that when we lose, it is good for us, and better things are on the way. Let us develop the attitude that when God closes a door, he has planned something better for us.

Self-action Plan

Actions   **By When**

1.

2.

3.

Review after Three Months

Be True to Yourself

The privilege of a lifetime is to become who you truly are.

— C G Jung

It is important to be true to yourself. All leaders have this quality. People sometimes try to pretend to be what they are not. They do this because they want to look good in the eyes of others. Other reasons could be ego, fear of being vulnerable, not wanting to lose, not accepting defeat, to cheat, or fear of being judged, fear of what others may think or something else. So, people wear masks to show themselves as different.

Ramakrishna Paramahamsa was a great teacher. Though he was not educated, a lot of people would come to him for advice. One day, a mother came to him saying that her son was eating too much jaggery. The guru told the mother to return a few days later with the boy. When she did, Ramakrishna told the boy not to eat jaggery. The mother was surprised and asked him as to why he didn't do say this when they came to him the first time. Ramakrishna told her that he also loved to eat jaggery. So first, he had to stop the habit before he told her son to do so. Ramakrishna was true to himself. He could have pretended to be above bad habits. He did not do so.

Our conflict comes when we speak what we do not mean. I have seen people saying yes to something when what they really mean is no. This mismatch does not make us comfortable and we struggle to keep up our image.

People like to look good to others basically. Divorces happen when one partner pretends to be someone they are not, all the time, and one day it shows. One of my friends once admitted that he used to pretend that he understood everything presented by his juniors at office. He did not want to admit his ignorance before his juniors. Circumstances made him realise that putting on a mask would not work, and he the developed the ability to ask questions when he did not know something. His relationships with his juniors is better now.

Once we stop pretending to be who we are not, our relationships with others improves, people will approach us more freely, and will feel comfortable dealing with us. Our image will certainly improve.

Let us ask following questions to ourselves:

1. Am I pretending to be someone?

2. Why am I doing that?

3. What benefit am I getting by pretending to be this way?

4. What penalty am I paying because of this?

Let us try to be true to ourselves. Shall we share with our nearest friend or relative, one act of pretence we are doing in order to look good?

Self-action Plan

Actions   **By When**

1.

2.

3.

Review after Three Months

The Beginning of Learning

Education is not the learning of facts, but the training
of the mind to think.

– Albert Einstein

There was an expert teacher of karate. Learning from him was tough. It used to take years for students under him to move from being a white belt to the level of a black belt. In the world of karate, the black belt is considered as the peak of expertise. One student was on the verge of getting his black belt. He was eagerly looking forward to his certificate.

One day, the teacher said, "I want to test your mental maturity and your physical development. What is the purpose of getting the black belt?" The student thought this to be a silly question. He replied that getting a black belt was the ultimate test of learning and was testimony to years of hard work. The teacher fell silent. He later told the student that the he was not qualified for the black belt as yet, and that he should practice for one more year. At the end of the one year, the teacher asked him the same question. This time, the student answered, "The black belt is an indication that I have reached the peak of my skills."

The teacher was not satisfied again. The student had to learn for one more year. At the end of the year, the same question was posed. This time, the student said, "Getting a black belt is not the end of learning. It is the beginning of learning – how to apply in the real world what I learnt in class." This time, he got his certificate.

Students should not think that by graduating, they know it all. In fact, their learning in real life has just begun. My message to the out-going final year engineering students in an engineering college was, "Your journey in college ends by getting an engineering degree. But when you step out into the real world, you start as trainees."

We need to decide whether we want an engineering degree or want to be an engineer. That decides where you begin or end your learnings.

Self-action Plan

Actions	By When
1.	
2.	
3.	

Review after Three Months

Take Risks

If you don't take risks, you will always work for someone who does.
– Dhirubhai Ambani

There are two types of people – one believes that taking risks is not at all good. For the other, risk-taking is a way of life. The approach towards risk depends on one's upbringing. "No risk, no gain" is a saying. Personally I believe that there cannot be growth without risks. But it should be a calculated risk. How do we get this calculation right?

There are two aspects in this calculation. One is, what is the probability of the event considered as risky happening? If that event does happen, what is the impact? The multiplication of these two aspects gives a sort of risk number.

Assume that there is a pit 10 feet wide, with a depth of 8 feet. If someone is asked to jump across this pit, would he do it? If he is already a long jumper and has cleared 12 feet earlier, he might take the chance. Otherwise anyone would hesitate to take the risk as the probability of a fall is high.

Richard Branson, who started the Virgin Group of companies said, "Brave may not live forever. But the cautious do not live at all." He took a lot of risks getting into many ventures, and ended with control of more than 350 companies. He says that without taking risks, no business will take shape or flourish. One should have belief in himself and commit 100% to the business, is his view.

William C Miller, the internationally-recognised expert on values-centred innovation has developed an innovative process. In this process, he identifies eight steps to innovate anything. The first step is to set the intention. This is to be clear about what exactly we what to do. It could be for example, starting a business. He recommends in the second step, to assess the risks involved. Normally, this step is ignored and we go ahead with the business, overlooking the risks. During the stage of risk assessment, we should list down what could go wrong. The moment we think of risks, our confidence level will go down. To bring back the confidence level, he recommends the third step, to tap into our character. This step is to bring back the inner strength to overcome the risks listed. In this process, we would assess the risks and be ready with the actions to overcome the risks.

Failure to consider uncertainty and risks will lead to continual fire-fighting. In the worst case, it will lead to a crisis. In the end, we only regret the chances we didn't take or attempt. To summarise, taking risks itself is not bad. But your assessment of risks with readiness of action is better.

Where can we take a risk now, to grow?

Self-action Plan

Actions   **By When**

1.

2.

3.

Review after Three Months

Being at the Right Place

There is never just one thing that leads to success for anyone. I feel it always a combination of passion, dedication, hard work and being in the right place at the right time.

– Lauren Conrad

For success, being smart and intelligent is not enough. We need to be at the right place where our talent and intelligence is respected and nourished. Without that, our full potential will not be exploited. I have seen many people getting stuck in the wrong places. Because they do not want to leave their comfort zone, they are not willing to change place as well.

In a zoo garden, a baby camel asked its mother, "Mummy, why do we have long eyelashes?" The mother camel explained how the long eyelashes prevented sand from getting into their eyes, in desert conditions. This, she explained, helps the camel survive in the desert. The baby camel's next question was about the hump. His mother explained how the hump helped conserve water so that they could survive in the arid desert. The curious baby went on with to ask, "Mummy, why do we have wide feet?" The mother explained how their wide feet helped them walk easily on sand. The baby camel was happy with all the three answers but then he frowned. His next question came soon. "Mummy," he said, "God has given us all our features to help us survive in a desert. What are we doing here, in a zoo garden?" The mother had no answer.

I am not suggesting change for the sake of it. It is important to introspect whether the place we are in helps us achieve our goals of life.

Will it support to bring out the best in me? Will it become a platform to demonstrate my strengths? Am I stuck here with few options? Should I look for new options? Is it worth spending time here? Is the comfort level holding me back so much that I am unable to leave? Am I considering opportunities lying outside my comfort zone?

Remember that opportunities always lie outside our comfort zones.

Self-action Plan

Actions	By When
1.	
2.	
3.	

Review after Three Months

Benefits from Yoga

Yoga means addition – addition of energy, strength
and beauty to body, mind and soul.

– Amit Ray

The epic *Ramayana* is a great source for many lessons in life. Each incident in the story reflects the many facets of human behaviour. We know the story of the *Ramayana* by now. How Rama was exiled by his step-mother, Sita kidnapped by Ravana, and how Rama rescues her from Lanka. There is a parallel between the *Ramayana* and what happens in our body.

Each main character here can be linked to yogic principles. Lord Rama personifies the Soul or bigger SELF. He is an icon to demonstrate how one can aspire for perfection. Sita reflects the mind, which is always wavering. She wanted the golden deer despite Lakshmana's warning. She just wanted the golden deer. This led to a series of events ending in the battle at Lanka. Lord Hanuman signifies breath. This is apt as well since Hanuman is the son of Vaayu (Air). Hanuman struggles to unite Rama and Sita.

Lakshmana reflects awareness. He supports Rama and Sita throughout the events that unfurl. Ravana personifies ego. He did not want to listen to anyone. Good advice from brother Vibhishana fell on deaf ears. Ravana ruined himself thanks to his ego.

If we link the characters of Ramayana to that of yoga, we see that the Soul (Rama) is united with the mind (Sita) with the help of breath (Hanuman) and supported by Awareness (Lakshmana) to get rid of ego (Ravana). Yoga is nothing but the unification of the individual self (*Jivatma*) with that of universal SELF (*Paramatma*). This unification process can be achieved by our eight limbs as prescribed by the seer Patanjali, about 4,000 years ago. Popularly known as Ashtanga Yoga, it involves our limbs which follow the *Yama* (disciplines), *Niyama* (injunctions), *Asana* (postures of the body), *Pranayama* (control of breath), *Prathyahara* (restraint of the senses), *Dhyana* (meditation), *Dharana* (concentration) and *Samadhi* (Super Consciousness).

Practising yoga helps in healthy living, better emotional handling and enhanced relationships with others. Learning yoga could be the starting point for students to gain value-based education. The benefit of yoga comes only if practised daily and becomes a way of life. It has nothing to do with religion and anyone can practice it.

Are we ready to practice yoga?

Self-action Plan

Actions   **By When**

1.

2.

3.

Review after Three Months